Laughing
in the Kitchen

The Streetfeet Women, a culturally diverse company of writers and performers, was founded in Boston in 1982 by Mary Millner McCullough and Elena Harap. The group creates theatre based on the writings of its members, celebrating the dignity and creativity with which ordinary women live their lives.

Streetfeet performs in places where women live and work—in neighborhood libraries, community centers, prisons, schools, colleges, and churches, as well as regional conferences. In 1985 the company traveled to Nairobi, Kenya, to take part in the Non-Governmental Organizations (NGO) Forum of the United Nations Decade for Women Conference. While in Kenya they toured their show "Many Voices." In 1995 they journeyed to China to perform "All in a Woman's Family" at the NGO Forum of the U.N. Fourth World Conference on Women in Huairou. The group published journals of their adventures at these two world conferences.

Streetfeet's experiences at home and abroad have given the members a deeper understanding of their identity as American women. The company's 1998 production, "American Praise Song," scripted by Mary McCullough and based upon material from **Laughing in the Kitchen**, reflects their search for the heart and soul of America.

Their work has been supported by private donors and by the Boston Arts Lottery, the Massachusetts Council on the Arts and Humanities, Polaroid Foundation, the Boston Globe Foundation, the Cambridge River Festival, the Parker Hill Library, the Somerville Public Library, and the Boston Women's Fund.

Laughing in the Kitchen

SHORT STORIES, POEMS, ESSAYS, AND MEMOIRS

by

The Streetfeet Women

BLANCA E. BONILLA, ELENA HARAP,
MARY MILLNER McCULLOUGH,
LI MIN MO, AURA LUZ SANCHEZ

TALKING STONE PRESS

BOSTON

ISBN 0-944941-12-5

Mailing address: The Streetfeet Women, c/o M. McCullough, 30 Brastow Avenue, Somerville, MA 02143

Also by The Streetfeet Women:

Many Voices, Streetfeet Publications, 1988
The Road to Beijing (with other authors), Streetfeet Publications, 1996

Text edited by Elena Harap

Translations by Blanca E. Bonilla and Yarice Hidalgo, with Elena Harap and Aura Luz Sanchez

Cover illustration and graphics by Geraldine McCullough

Book design by Deborah Bluestein

Talking Stone Press promotes a richer understanding of the Language Arts through poetry, music, and song while supporting the appreciation of diverse cultural expression. Call 1-800-557-3100 for a free catalogue.

Printing by BookMasters

Versions of works in this collection first appeared in the following:

Elena Harap: "Roxbury Sister Blues," Sojourner; "Maryanne Without Makeup," Womanblood, ed. O'Brien, Rasmussen & Costello, Continuing Saga Press, 1981; "Talk to Us About Salvation," Many Voices, Streetfeet, 1988; "Restoration Crew at the Burial Ground," "April 1968," "Post Modern Mom," Out of the Kitchen; "Post Modern Mom," "She Prays," "April 1968," NPR Station WFCR, Amherst, Mass.

Mary Millner McCullough: "Outbound," Out of the Kitchen.

Li Min Mo: "A Bundle of Laundry Notes," Sampan; excerpts from "A Journey in Search of My Voice," The Road to Beijing, Streetfeet, 1996; "What Fay-Yen Carries Across the Pacific," Poetpourri.

Aura Luz Sanchez: "The Schoolyard," Out of the Kitchen; "Mami," Paradise, ed. Childrey, Meece & Sink, Florida Literary Foundation Press, 1993.

*This book is dedicated to our families
with everlasting thanks
for their love and encouragement.*

Acknowledgments

To our coaches Marjorie Agosín and Laurie Alberts, who nurtured this book. • To our teachers and friends—Martín Espada, Josephine Lane, Lynda Patton, and James Spruill. • To Geraldine McCullough, Judith Steinbergh, Elizabeth McKim, Deborah Bluestein, Joy Wallens-Penford, Terri Ziter, Joan Chater Harap, Marilyn Britt, Betsy Lenke, Mary Burton, Peggy Keller, Ruth O'Meara, Roxana Laughlin, Aaron Bluestein, and all of our supporters who made this book a reality.

AURA: To my husband, Frank, for his strength and unfailing support. To my parents, Elisa and Toñito, who lived my stories, my sister, Virginia, who helped resurrect them, my children, Dylan, Seth, and Anelisa, who will inherit them, and to my brother, Ramón.

BLANCA: To my mother, María Veléz de Bonilla, for her strength and guidance, to my father, Rafael Bonilla García, for his loyalty and tolerance, and to my son, Ramón Burgos, for his respect and support.

ELENA: To my Harap sisters, Linda, Joan, and Eileen, and to all my other sisters; to Ted Dodd, and our children, Eben and Angie; to Kathleen Spivack.

LI MIN: In memory of my mother, Diana Hsu Chin; to my family: Dan Lenke, Cho San Mo, Yuing Mo, Li San Mo. To Dewitt Henry: he believed in me and cultivated my reading mind; to Joyce Peseroff; to Kathleen Anderson; to Bill Knott.

MARY: In memory of my mom, Nannie H. Millner, and my high school English teacher, Mrs. Johnson. Thank you to Skip, Kim, and Scott McCullough for their support and technical assistance with the computer. A special appreciation to my dad, Frank Millner, for telling his story first, and to my brother, Frank, Jr., and sister, Lynn, for the adventures we shared in our childhood.

Contents

Introduction

I Tending the Fire

II Testimonies

III. Incantations

IV. Mu Shi / Mother Stream

ABOUT THE AUTHORS

Blanca E. Bonilla was born in Lares, Puerto Rico, the ninth of thirteen children. At thirteen, she moved to Boston with her family. She attended Wheelock College and acted with Boston Youtheatre, Teatro Acción, El Pueblo Nuevo, and Streetfeet. Blanca works as a Family Coordinator at the Maurice J. Tobin School in Mission Hill, Boston, and directs the Tobin School Family Theatre Program. She is an outspoken advocate for girls' participation in sports.

Elena Harap, descended from Northern European immigrants, grew up in Tennessee and lives in Vermont. She holds degrees from Wellesley College and Boston University, and studied acting with Linda Putnam, June Judson, New African Company, and Josephine Lane. Work with People's Theatre of Cambridge led to the co-founding of Streetfeet Workshops, supported by Polaroid and Globe Foundations, Mass. Council on the Arts and Humanities, and Boston Arts Lottery. She studied with Laurie Alberts, Martín Espada, and Kathleen Spivack. With support from the American Association of University Women, Polaroid Foundation, and the Vermont Council on the Humanities, she wrote and now performs "Meet Eleanor Roosevelt," directed by co-author Josephine Lane.

Mary Millner McCullough, of African-American and Cherokee descent, was born in Virginia and lives in Somerville, Mass. She studied theatre arts at Goddard College and acted with the People's Theatre of Cambridge, Mass. She coordinates a busing program that brings inner-city children of color to a Boston suburban school. The Anti-Defamation League recognized Mary for her work against discrimination and prejudice. A grant from the Weston Education Enrichment Fund Committee funded her play, "'Goin' to the Promise Land," based on study of the Great Migration at the W. E. B. DuBois Institute, Harvard University. Mary is a member of the Dramatists Guild and is pursuing a Master of Arts in Writing at Northeastern University.

Born in Shanghai, Li Min Mo immigrated to America at thirteen and lives in Cambridge, Mass. She trained at Reality Theatre in Boston, studied with Kathleen Spivack, and holds an M.A. in Theatre and Education from Goddard College and an M.F.A. from Emerson College. Her poetry has appeared in journals and anthologies. A storyteller and teacher of Chinese culture, with funding from Mass. Cultural Council, Chapter 636 Grants, and Cambridge Arts Council, Li Min received a grant from Channel 4's "You Gotta Have Arts" for her play "Mending the Sky." A 1997 Barbara Deming "Money for Women" Fund poetry grant recipient, she also exhibits art work in galleries and is on the adjunct faculty at Lesley College.

Aura Luz Sanchez was born in the South Bronx to Puerto Rican parents living in one of the oldest barrios in New York City. She lives in Winthrop, Mass. Aura studied sociology and anthropology at Brooklyn College of the City University of New York. She holds an M.A. in Education from Harvard University and a law degree from Northeastern University. She is a trained mediator and has worked as a public interest lawyer. She is Director of Health and Human Services for the city of Chelsea, Mass. Aura studied writing with Yusef Komunyakaa and Martín Espada at the Joiner Center, University of Massachusetts. She has been a guest reader in workshops for Boston high school students.

Introduction

STREETFEET, AMERICAN-NESS, AND DANGER

*On July 12, 1994, the authors of this book gathered around Mary
McCullough's dining room table to talk about how they came together as
writers, using questions from writing coach Marjorie Agosín. The following is
an excerpt from the conversation that ensued.*

ELENA HARAP: Streetfeet came out of my friendship with
Angela Cook. I grew up in Nashville, Tennessee; she grew up
in Richmond, Virginia, and our paths crossed in Roxbury,
Massachusetts. We got hired by the city to do outdoor theatre workshops with kids. One day in my kitchen Angela saw a game,
"Streetfeet," my son had made with a friend and said, "Why don't we
call the workshops Streetfeet?" Out on the street, we were creating
a "civic culture." It reflected my immigrant background, where people come with a rich heritage and want to create something that
wasn't there already—like Streetfeet, when five kids chose to be
Cinderella's fairy godmother. We just changed the story and she got
five godmothers. [*Laughter*]

Mary and I first met in the Sixties, in the People's Theatre.
Later we talked about taking a performance to the 1985 Decade for
Women Conference in Nairobi. We gathered a group and named it
the Streetfeet Women's Touring Company. After the Conference,
this nucleus of women continued to meet. The interest of the group
in things that are close to me, such as trying to help my mother
have a good life in her last years, led me to writing that rang true.
Marjorie Agosín's saying "Introduce yourself" opened a well of
memory; it was all coming out of my hand onto the page. I was once
told that if you are very public, there's always the opposite in you,
very private, and it's that balance that keeps you healthy and
integrated.

LI MIN MO: Elena and I did Streetfeet theatre workshops with kids

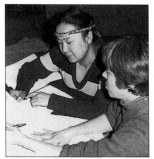

in Boston after I had spent a couple of years in theatre training. I taught ESL in Chinatown, but at that time they paid very little. I started getting story-telling jobs. The minute I dealt with stories, I had to deal with writing. "Don't make me write—it's torture!" I would scribble it so I couldn't read it, and I'd have to scribble it again.

If Streetfeet didn't like my first pieces, they would say, "Bring your second stuff over." There was a lot of generosity in the group, allowing me a period of hibernation—producing poetry and stories, not sending work anywhere, slowly cultivating my self-esteem.

I've been a performer since I was three. Writing has helped me. With performing, I always felt, "Oh, I don't look good today, my dress is ugly . . ." But writing is so simple; it speaks, once it's finished.

BLANCA BONILLA: Streetfeet kind of rescued me, remember? I had just separated from Ramón's father. Elena called me up, she said you needed a Latino person. I wanted to do theatre. Streetfeet gave me a space that I felt comfortable in. Many times I would question myself, "Oh, I should be having fun with the young girls" [laughter]—but for many reasons I stayed with the group. We have a vision of women in society and we take energy from each other. We try to plant that seed in our own communities so that things will be different when our girls grow up—or when the girls of our girls grow up.

In Latino women's groups I feel good because I identify with them, I can understand where they come from. And over here I also feel good. It's like changing TV channels, being in the middle of two worlds, two different cultures. Sometimes you need more from one channel than from another. Am I making myself clear? [Laughter, agreement]

AURA LUZ SANCHEZ: Before I met you all, although I knew Mary in a different context, I never had contact with people who thought of themselves as performers, artists, or writers. I was practicing law. Streetfeet opened a way of writing not in isolation, brought it out of the closet. Jo Lane's feedback in our performance coaching sessions helped; she said, "You know, I just heard you yelling at your son, and you don't use that tiny, tinny voice when you yell at your son." It was some kind of an epiphany because she was tapping into the real me, that was not self-conscious, that was out there yelling at Seth, as opposed to a different me that is more protective. As a child I was extremely shy—I would dig into my mother's skirt and try to hide at the thought of having to meet people. Writing is a way that I can say anything and do anything.

In some way we are creative anthropologists, saying who we are in a culture that's changing and multifaceted, that is—for me—between being Puerto Rican and American, married to a Jew, and having gone to a Catholic school that was ninety-nine per cent Irish. We grow up with the notion that everything has to be linear and goal-oriented. Many lives don't go that way, certainly less so for women than for men. We do have to spend time taking care of our mothers or our husbands or at home with our kids. I don't see it as "We're out of the mainstream." That experience becomes the material this group is so comfortable tapping into. Streetfeet is like this crucible or this petri dish: anything could come out of it!

MARY: Streetfeet gives me an opportunity to define myself. In other places I am someone else's projection of who I should be. The role of wife and mother is sort of determined, if not by the people around you, then by what you grew up thinking it should be. I'd always wanted to write—at one of the first orientation meetings at Goddard College the president said, "What are you going to major in?" I said, "Journalism!" He said, "You're in the wrong school. We don't have journalism here." All the way from Virginia, I'd gotten into this interesting school, and they didn't have journalism? There was emphasis on writing there, but I've never done what I want to do. Sometimes voices come to me demanding that their stories be told. Once I name a story after a woman, she tells me what her story is.

I would like to leave a legacy for my family, all those who struggled so hard. For me as a colored person in America—and I like that term because it lends itself to all the various mixtures—it's important. I want to validate their courage by writing about the lives of women, children, and men.

There are two questions we want to deal with now: *What is your American-ness?* and *In what part of your writing do you find a sense of danger?*

LI MIN: I'm writing in English, but not classical, perfect English. The fact that all I have is broken English speaks everything about what America meant for me. Chinese, Hispanics, all the people I grew up with in New York, had just broken-up English. How it becomes their language is important. When I went to Africa I said, I am an American woman and I do not want to be any other kind of woman. I realized that here I have the freedom to create an American persona.

AURA: For many years I accentuated the fact that I'm a minority, a Puerto Rican. When I lived in Peru, I was struck by how American my thinking is. We fall into the trap of defining America as mainstream, white, Anglo society. I'd like to redefine America to be what we are, and not buy into something that makes us comfortable because we can then be different and have something to be angry at.

MARY: I was angry that someone would dare ask me this question. I've always felt on the outside of whatever this "American" thing is. But I value the idea of America, of democracy. When someone wants to see me as the "other," I laugh to myself now and think, "You know, what *you're* trying to do doesn't belong."

BLANCA: When I was thirteen I came to Boston and hated this place. I would say, "Wait until I'm eighteen, I'm leaving." I am still here! I love Puerto Rico. I thought about living there. I speak the language very well and understand the culture. Although women there are getting educated and going on to college, the *machismo* is expressed and accepted differently from the U.S. Here it's more diplomatic; you don't hear so clearly as you hear it there. American men deny it, but they really practice it.

I feel very proud of being Puerto Rican, but I have built a life in Boston. I belong to both worlds. My mother will say, "*Oh, es porque estas tan americanizada*"—it is because you are so americanized! I'm happy where I'm standing right now.

ELENA: At the Women's Conference in Nairobi a big globe was inscribed, "As a woman I have no country—my country is the world." I think you can believe that and still identify with your country. When my son was in Little League I thought, "I'm really American now. He's playing the national game. The immigrants came over the ocean for something like this."

MARY: I want to say something about American-ness and language: Americans don't speak standard English. That's a myth. The language we're taught in school is the language of the marketplace, and we learn it to move in the marketplace. I guess it's part of being in mid-life and growing older, you start thinking, "Oh. That's not real." Americans speak the way *we* speak—now, yesterday, and tomorrow.

LI MIN: In what part of writing do you find a sense of danger—spirituality. My mother, a super-educated woman, said, "People who are uneducated worship gods, they light incense. You see all those women going to that festival: they are lowly people, and we're not one of them." I shut up that part of me. Later I began to get in touch with it. In the Chinese community, one half will say, "She's wacko," and the other says, "She's just like us! We believe in all the ghosts and spirits we worship."

AURA: Not so much dangerous as difficult is writing about people we know well. When I think I've captured some part of a person, the next moment I'm saying, "Oh, but this person is completely different in these situations"—like a kaleidoscope. I don't want to present them in simplistic ways.

LI MIN: Mary, when you name the story after one of your relatives and the story possesses you, a lot of writers would call that the Muse. Religious people for centuries have been calling it the creative dark power that has a shamanic origin, and it is a possession.

MARY: You could be correct, I *am* being possessed by whatever this is, and that's dangerous!

LI MIN: Yes, it's dangerous and exciting.

Transcription from audio tape by Cathy Lauden, edited by Elena Harap

PHOTOGRAPHS FROM AUTHORS' PRIVATE COLLECTIONS

Frontispiece: The Streetfeet Women in Mary's dining room, Somerville, Mass., 1994. Left to right, Aura Luz Sanchez, Mary Millner McCullough, Li Min Mo, Elena Harap, Blanca Bonilla. Photo by Michael McLaughlin.

Introduction

STREETFEET, AMERICAN-NESS, AND DANGER, page viii: Li Min and Elena, Boston, 1983.

Tending the Fire

A JOURNEY IN SEARCH OF MY VOICE, page 3: Li Min, age fifteen, New York City.

FEBRUARY SEVENTEENTH, page 37: Blanca, age seventeen, on her wedding day.

RAMÓN, page 39: Blanca's son Ramón, age two weeks.

TO LIVE IN THE MARGINS, page 50: Aura,1944, the Bronx; page 54: Aura's parents, Toñito and Elisa.

Testimonies

REACHING DREAMS, page 76: Blanca, third from left, with team members Lissette, Iris, and Desiree.

NIGHT RIVER, page 84: Li Min in the 1970s, Cambridge, Mass.

IMBROGLIO, page 88: Charity Christian Church, Martinsville, Virginia.

IN THE WILDERNESS, page 100: Mary, age five, at right, with her sister Lynn; page 114: Mary, age seventeen, in Virginia.

COSAS DE LA NOCHE/THINGS OF THE NIGHT, page 116: Blanca's parents with their oldest daughter, Amelia.

Incantations

WORDS AS MAGICAL INCANTATIONS, page 127: Elena, at left, with her sisters Linda, Eileen, and Joan, circa 1944; page 132: Elena's father's family, the Haraps, circa 1908; page 136: Elena's great-grandmother, Harriet Naylor, with her mother, Norah Joan Chater, circa 1902.

DOUBLE DUTCH ON EAST 152ND STREET, page 146: Aura, age three, in her parents' apartment, East 152nd Street.

BACK COVER PHOTO CREDITS:

Brooks Brown: Elena Harap
Richard Chase: Mary Millner McCullough, Li Min Mo, Aura Luz Sanchez
Michael McLaughlin: Blanca Bonilla

Tending the Fire

Li Min Mo

A JOURNEY
IN SEARCH OF MY VOICE

Excerpt from a memoir in progress

When I write I stumble on words because they have such power over me, over my memories, over my life. Sometimes, waking up to write, I feel like a night-thief stealing a moment to be with the moon, or journeying to the stars alone, leaving my kids behind. The trauma of war years, poverty, motherhood severed the coherent narrative of my inner voice. However, in the low hum of my computer I have discovered a trusted medium. Words are bones, ingredients for medicine. Writing heals. For decades I was absorbed in images; personalized movies reeled through my waking mind and my dreams at night. Only recently have I begun to grapple with words and the way they too, like old photo albums, can verify my memories.

My life began with simple images. Shanghai, 1947-1952: At dawn, shuffling in my slippers, I went into the kitchen. Where was mother? I was hungry and it was so chilly I could see my breath, feel my ears getting numb. I wiped my fingers on the window pane. I saw mother wearing an old silk robe; the golden threads were frayed, but still shimmered brightly. Bits of silk padding stuck out; tiny embroidered red blossoms with green leaves glowed like tiny lanterns. Bending low, she shredded newspaper, stuffed it into a small hibachi. Shrouded in smoke, she looked like a Buddha with offerings. She fanned the flame with a split yellow palm fan; sparks flew like stars and snow started to come down. Mother opened an umbrella; it looked like a giant flower holding the sky. Thousands of snowflakes hovered around my Fire Keeper. I opened the door, looked up and saw a sky so full and blinding; smoke of the fire rose to a faceless heaven. Then we had hot porridge, hot face cloth, a warm kitchen. Every morning I delighted in ordinary magic.

A year later, people were shouting on the street. A fire truck pulled up near our house. Suddenly I heard a lot of neighbors yelling, "Grandfather, don't jump. Please, we beg you . . . ." I saw an old man with a long gray beard, wearing a long white gown. In a flash he leapt off the roof; a shaft of sunlight embraced him. The crowd was shocked, as if something monstrous had shaken the root of its life. The firemen covered everything with white cloth, but they left a small pool of blood on the concrete. At age three I discovered "blank-out" stares in my neighbors' eyes. For days no one wanted to look down, look up, or look inside. In the heat of summer nights I dreamed about the sleeves of a white nightgown flying to the sky. I woke up haunted by a faceless ghost, my toes awash in moonlight, and I prayed for all that was constant. Looking outside my window, I discovered a sky filled with beckoning stars, disappearing and coming into being.

That winter the soldiers marched, shaking our window panes. Their steps inflamed the frozen ground. Their unison shouts pierced our hearts. We peeked out from our windows and saw two soldiers scolding and pushing Mrs. Wong around when she was caught sacrificing a chicken to honor her husband's death. The poor woman was shaking, whimpering like an injured dog, holding her fowl upside-down by its feet. She pleaded, "For the spirits' sake . . . the spirit of the dead." A near-dead fowl, its red wings flapping, its blood splattering on all the walls, appeared in my dreams. Loud shrieks. I heard the soldiers coming to get me in the dark; I grabbed my throat and thought of the neck of a chicken.

Some days there were still moments of fun. My sisters taught me the Mongolian dance. Accompanied by one sister banging on a tambourine and the other three roaring like wild horses, I pretended that I was a princess of the steppes. A brass band interrupted our play. From our windows we saw trombones that looked like elephant trunks; the musicians all wore military uniforms, while the mourners wore white burlap gowns; they marched with their hoods bobbing. Why were they wailing? My feet tapped to the sound of their march. I spun around and saw a vase with budding magnolias. It reminded me of the inviting music. "Mama, can I wail and holler like them? Can I join the parade?" When mother went upstairs, I sneaked out. The street was empty. Mr. Lau's door was ajar, incense smoke smothering in his hall. I leaned on his doorframe. At the end of the hall stood a long, dark box. I wanted to go in and take a good look at it. Waiting for courage, listening to the rapid beating of my own heart, I hummed the tune I had overheard that morning. A darkness descended on everything; the black box grew bigger. I climbed up a stone step and tripped over it, banging my head, knocking myself unconscious. I lay in a coma for weeks; mother thought I would not return. A Mask of Death shadowed my life, but my soul was still humming grace notes of the mourning song, keeping time with the beating of my heart.

Shortly after I got home from the hospital and learned how to move like a normal kid again, trouble started visiting our home. For days I would wake up and find non-uniformed government people sitting around our living room interrogating my father. I guessed that my father didn't give them the information they were looking for. Finally one morning three non-uniformed soldiers came up to our door. Their menacing stares, or maybe the coldness in their voices, signaled that they were sent to our house to do something terrible to my father. I had to put up a fight with these strangers; at age three I had not had fear beaten into me. Sprawling on the ground in front of our house, I wrapped my arms tightly around my father's pants legs. The three soldiers stared down at me while admonishing my mother, who was pleading with them. They dragged my father away from my grip. I remember those men's words: "We need to have a talk with Mr. Mo. We want him to tell us what he knows. We'll let him go." They put my father into the prison. My mother was not allowed to see him or deliver a toothbrush and blanket to him.

Our electricity was shut off. Our pantry emptied. Each day another piece of furniture was taken to the pawn shop. The Singer sewing machine and the console radio became the last things to go. The walls around us grew taller. Many months after my father was incarcerated, my mother heard his voice: first he knocked on our door, and later he called her name from the rooftop. That night my father appeared in my mother's dream. Soldiers were marching alongside hundreds of political prisoners on their way to execution; someone pointed him out to my mother and said, "Go take a last look at your husband." My mother caught a glimpse of my father, his head dropping to his chin, hands tied behind his back, scruffy, with an unshaven face. When my mother woke, she asked my sister to go get a newspaper. On the headline was a long list of political prisoners, and my father's name was among many that had fallen. (More than four decades later, the government apologized to my mother for its wrongful execution of my father.)

My mother was not allowed to mourn, or even to dress in the proper attire of the newly widowed. Every day she had to go to confession meetings to criticize herself and confess her family's wrongdoings. And she reminded us, "No one is allowed to light incense, say a prayer. No one is allowed to go outside after dark. There are eyes watching everywhere." Inside the belly of a Dark Dragon we went on scratching out a living. If I had known some forms of prayer, I would have said this for my five-year-old self: *Let me not shut my eyes; seeing is drawing courage. Let me not forget the small joys of my body in a warm tub, in the arms of my mother. Let me always feel my body's way of knowing; in the midst of pain, fever, nightmares, there are healing touches, soothing voices, warm quilts, a room filled with light. Let me possess courage and faith as if they are two limbs of my body.*

Every day, while washing dishes or scrubbing laundry, my mother frantically repeated, "*Your father has been executed and what should I do, commit suicide?* War, eight foreign nations carved up Shanghai; Japanese ghosts burned our homes, *tow-nan—escape from war and bombing raids, all these orphans, tso-toe-may-lu—at my wit's end—without a road ahead, sze-ma-feng-sze—a body being pulled apart by four horses, aiiie, ku-min—bitter fate!*" Her words became my nightmares. My blockage of words began. A fortune teller told my mother, "You can never get out of this doomed world—a poor widow with a lot of kids. You will drown in the bitter sea. Have you forgotten the well-known phrase, 'Widows and little orphans are worse than garbage'?" Mother corrected the old soothsayer, "The phrase is, 'People loathe and despise widows and orphans.'" After attending weekly confession meetings, my mother realized the Communists' revolution would be carried out with years of "re-education" and "eating bitterness." She decided to brave all odds—to flee her birthplace, to smuggle her family to the land of freedom. It was impossible for her to bring along all her children, so she left my four older sisters with my grandmother and took the three youngest with her.

Before we left mainland China, we briefly stayed with my grandmother. In front of her dark entrance I smelled the chamber-pots and the raw sewage flowing in a ditch. After I climbed up a flight, entering through her door I was transported to an enchanting place. A long, red, wood table with carved legs and ornate trim around the side dominated the living room. I pulled open the big drawer and found a lot of seals. Miniature stone animal carvings stared at me with their strange expressions. Painted scrolls decorated the walls, two tall cabinets were filled with sculptures and curios, even the porcelain stools were carved and painted with scenes of gardens and people dressed in gowns from an ancient era.

I was not allowed to enter my grandmother's bedroom, a temple always smothered in incense. Large statues of Kuen Yin and Buddha stood on top of a mantel; red candle light shone on their benevolent expressions. Two cat-o'-nine-tails hung on one wall. A huge canopy bed occupied another side of the room. My grandmother's kitchen was a living thing in my memory; like her bedroom, it was a place that I was not allowed to enter. I stood outside and peeked at the coal stove in one corner, a large tin basin filled with water for washing, bamboo baskets of various sizes hanging on the wall, sausages and pieces of salted meat hanging from the low rafters. A small stool made with bamboo and wood, shaped by my grandmother's bottom, caught my eye. One day I sneaked into the small, dark kitchen and rubbed my hands on that stool. I sat on it and pretended that I was a grandmother, preparing eels, salting meat, chopping vegetables with a cleaver on a big stump of a tree.

My grandmother was short. She had a face shaped like the moon, with many lines. When she smiled, I could see the inside of her mouth with only a few teeth left. Thin strands of white hair were pulled back into a small bun. She always wore black pants and a Chinese shirt, the kind that buttoned on the right side of her round figure. She came to see us off at the train station. My mother carried my little brother on her back, as well as a few bundles. The trains, "fire-vehicles," darkened by smoke and fogged by steam, loomed like monsters. Loud whistles blasted our ears. After we settled in our seats, we saw my grandmother rush toward our window. She handed my mother a big bundle wrapped with a handkerchief. Animal cookies. As tears welled in our eyes, we waved goodbye. I watched her small figure hobble away. My grandmother was bending over; her feet were smaller than my five-year-old's hands. She could not walk straight; her mother had bound her feet since she was five, or three, hoping the "golden lotus" would fetch her a well-off husband. I remember staring at the awkward, crippled image; it stabbed me with the suffering of Chinese women.

While changing trains, we stayed in a nearby inn. I woke up in the middle of the night and thought I heard an eerie cry. I crept outside, peeked down from the balcony, and saw a group of men gathering around a big table with a hole in the middle where a live monkey's head stuck out. One of the men took a knife, cut the monkey's head open, and took out its brain. Meantime, my mother suspected someone was following us; she decided to take off immediately. An image of the dead monkey dangled before me as we scurried out of the back door of the inn like thieves, or like animals escaping from a cage. We dozed off on the platform of the train station and waited for our next ride.

When we got off at the train station in Macau, we were surrounded by a huge, noisy crowd; on one side it was packed with "ocean devils" and on the other side filled with fearful, anxious Chinese. The shove and push in that hot summer day seemed to come from all directions. A single policeman tried to maintain order by blasting into the sky with his revolver, but no one paid him any attention. Eventually my mother pushed her way through and got us away from the crowd. The minute we caught our breath, we were surrounded by three men dressed in black. They spoke in a strange dialect. One guy grabbed me in his arms and the other guy snatched my brother. My mother kept talking calmly with the three gangsters as she followed them to a public telephone booth. I had never seen a phone before; the contraption looked so odd. My mother held the receiver, talking in a pleasant tone of voice. The three mean, sweaty, nervous-looking guys listened attentively. I thought the telephone was an instrument sent by the gods. We were saved. Within a short time we arrived at a mansion, my great-aunt's place, I was told. The elegant marble foyer with a marble spiral staircase and a huge chandelier dazzled me. Perhaps it was a dream; I held my breath. An old, gaunt woman descended the stairs. She wore a floor-length, silver satin ballroom gown. We learned that she was the proprietor of a gambling den and a ruler of the underworld.

I realized that aside from heaven and earth, there were many worlds, different rulers, oppressors, soldiers, gangsters, victims, alive, dead, caged, and free. Battles were not always fought with swords or guns. My mother was a warrior who knew how to communicate in many different tongues and how to journey from one world to another. I believed she possessed something powerful and had a third eye that watched over us.

We had to cross the sea to get to Hong Kong and freedom. The man who helped to smuggle us dressed us in black to mingle with the night. Each child was hidden inside an empty water barrel on a small sampan, accompanied by a boatman and boatwoman. My mother gave us treats; one brother got a rattle, the other got a fish toy, and I got a big red apple.

At age five I journeyed across the sea. It was a sweet summer night where everything was clearly drawn. In the dark, on the small boat, I held the apple like a lantern, the red lantern of celebration. My eyes closed, my body found the swaying rhythm of the sea as it had long ago inside my mother's womb. Everything was connected, the white foam floating like us; the world filled with wonder, danger and amazing powers; the sky with eyes and many faces; the sea with fish of bounty and life awaiting. The boatman smoked, dozed off, and dreamed while his wife paddled and sang. Then the wife drank hot tea and talked about fish prices while her husband turned the oars. I dreamed that a giant red-apple lantern guided the whole journey and the sea was a fishing couple who knew how to whistle to the stars and dance with the moon.

I later learned that my mother had to swim across the bay to board a cargo ship. Mother's faith was as deep as the sea. She must have prayed in the dark on the dangerous shore, tested the cold water with her feet, searched out the soldiers who watched throughout the night for stowaways. How did she climb aboard on that summer night? How did she find strength and courage while she scaled the slippery side of the cargo ship or grabbed on tight to the rope? Her children must have been her lifeline. She saw our faces, heard our voices, felt our breath in her bosom when she swam across the bay. In each stroke she must have held the only thing that could not be taken away from her—hope.

We settled in Hong Kong, moving from one slum dwelling to another. My mother's bravery and wits were my salvation. She was my lighthouse; she told me stories and read me poetry. But she could not suture my inner wounds; I was overwhelmed by a sense of futility. For my mother, that period was actually a freeing time; she wrote every day, getting stories into major Hong Kong newspapers and novels accepted by a publishing company.

In Hong Kong, where most people spoke Cantonese, I spoke only Mandarin. The two were completely different dialects. My mother was fluent in many dialects, including Cantonese, a skill she had acquired when she was a wartime reporter. I became withdrawn; my smiles look strained in pictures taken during those days. Too much had happened, too much had been taken away from me. Inside my little-girl self there was a soldier wanting to hate, to plunge in bloodshed. By age six I'd already witnessed not just death, but the savagery of humankind, the unspeakable atrocities human beings commit against each other. I felt the wrath of being human. I had nightmares of revenge: I would go on a killing rampage—an eye for an eye, a heart for a heart. In those dreams I was a boy, a man, a soldier without conscience, without a face, a murderer without language. How do soldiers describe the killing of helpless women and babies? Masters of war use words that make killing all right: *Defending Asia; Yellow Peril; Imperialist Running Dogs; Children of God.* Words that defend wars are like guns. Even "friendly fire" kills.

Although mother was a writer, I thought language belonged to men. Most authors I knew were men, so were philosophers, historians, scientists, composers, generals. My mother read to me often from her great collection of books. I loved to listen, but those great men's voices seemed to have no place in my little lot of squalor, poverty, and violence. I yearned for simple tales, small hopes, ordinary triumphs. Great literature had no place in an urban slum; most people were illiterate or read only newspapers, and older kids read only kung-fu novels. The great literature I was being introduced to didn't help me define my identity. In the predominantly male writers' community my mother was a rarity, a swan in a flock of dull-looking ducks.

My mother went to work, probably to a quiet place to write every day, and left me alone to defend myself. We lived behind a tailor shop. Our home was a small room that measured about ten by ten. The only furniture was a makeshift bed, a large board balanced on top of some boxes. The bathroom was a chamber pot; washing was done in a tin tub in the courtyard. I didn't feel safe in our small room or in the courtyard behind the building where everyone washed and sat around. Feeling totally helpless, I witnessed a tailor's apprentice chasing my youngest brother, beating him with a stick. I kept hearing neighbors berate us as dirty orphans, swearing that our life was dictated by bitter fate.

When I was six, a cook sexually abused me, which made me think my body was a piece of meat for that demonic man. He had the right to touch my private parts or shove his bulging penis into my hands. I didn't know as a little girl that I had any rights at all. Why didn't I tell my mother about those incidents? At the time I was afraid of the heavy-set, muscular cook living across the hall from us. I learned in a hard way what these words meant: widows and orphans are not protected. Bad Luck became my middle name. I accepted the notion that unlucky people with their ugly scabs and war wounds should not be out in the sun. I didn't know how to express my hurt in words, in common, everyday language. What were some of the words for my body's private parts in Chinese? I didn't know them and I was too scared to ask any big person. Our neighbors in the crowded tenement were a rowdy bunch of merchants, tailors, prostitutes, cooks; people with a narrow outlook of the world, people who were stuck within strict conventions, people who were most comfortable speaking slang.

I listened to the new language, slang and Cantonese, and after some years I came to understand a little; but when it was my turn to speak, my tongue was tied. The street kids had words; like the lowly peddlers, they spat out every phrase with racy offensives, "Fuck your mother, your granny, spray your stinking fart, eat dogshit." Their expressions didn't suit me; besides, boys were the ones who displayed their emotions unbashfully and felt comfortable talking about sexual experiences. One time an older boy told me, while rubbing his penis into a hard bone, that he was "shooting airplanes." I knew the slang for *penis*; for *vagina* there were obscure phrases I heard in poetry, like *dark corridor of the Ying*. *Preserving Yang essence* meant holding back ejaculation. Sexual intercourse was called *cloud-rain*.

I found out on my own that there was one kind of language for the educated and another for the uneducated. The uneducated used language that possessed action, animal power, and immediacy; their words maimed like weapons. My mother had mastered both languages. She could deliver an eloquent speech on the radio, quoting at ease passages from classical Chinese literature. When caught in a neighborhood dispute, she could defend herself by engaging in a hair-raising brawl. My mother could swear like the meanest gangster; I thought she had the power to turn her tongue into a cleaver and chop anyone trying to get in her way. I wanted a language that was visceral, empowering, liberating, but healing. All I discovered then was that there was no language for me; I was neither educated nor lowly.

I wished to be a street kid, a member of a gang, so that I could speak slang and claim a territory. I wanted to channel all my anger, deprivation, and despair into something awesome, fearful. I wanted a switchblade, a cigarette lighter, a thick belt, a good pair of leather shoes, tight-fitting clothes, loud gold rings, grease in my hair, money in my pockets and a fancy name like *White Bone, Dragon Fang, Shark Head*. Instead I was imprisoned in the persona of a mouse, a helpless creature with a squeaky voice. No gang would accept a girl. And kids called me Long-leg Crane. An ugly girl. I wished I were a boy; life would be more exciting. I could pee around the street corner, shout obscenities, collect trash, pick pockets, chew betel nuts, flex my muscles, and stick my chest out, topless. I imagined street kids' lives were filled with excitement and adventures. Years later, as an adult, when I had lived in different ghettos, I found out that street kids were usually bored, angry, and alienated, afraid to explore beyond the confines of their neighborhood. They felt stuck, with no future. Most of the time they had limited command of language. Theirs was a true broken narrative.

Not acquiring language, I developed my sensory awareness to perfection. I took mental notes in detail of things, sights, smells around me—the herbal brew everyone drank during the hottest days, smelly salves mother applied on my skin when I had rash, mumps. In the little, narrow kitchen where more than a dozen families took turns to cook, I heard the loud sound of spatulas hitting against woks. All I could see was a row of women bending over small kerosene stoves, skillfully sautéing or steaming their food. In that smoky place, they felt their way around as woman had done for thousands of years. The nights were long, buzzing with activity—women laughing, gossiping, playing mah-jong; men beating their children; kids stealing and then being rounded up by police; peddlers singing in a strange tongue; tired street performers, lugging their big trunks, heading home with their dogs and monkeys; a small hunchback girl whose mother carried her on her back. Her deformity and the way she clung to her mother's back haunt me to this day.

Holidays were rowdy, colorful, and endowed with many spirits. I loved the feverish Dragon Boat Festival along the bay, drummers on the helm, rowers' forceful arms, the crowd like countless waving flags, the heat burning through our heads, the fire of drumming in our hearts. In the Hungry Ghosts Festival, the whole street became a temple. Candles and dishes of cooked food lined the sidewalk. Worshipers burned piles of paper money, spirit gowns, spirit houses, and a big spirit boat—paraphernalia made of tissue paper. Countless little lanterns glowed on the dark street smothered in incense smoke. The worshipers believed everything they burned would reach heaven and their ancestors. A spirit world made tangible. Street kids taught me how to steal food and pennies from the ghosts: "You pray, bow, and ask for forgiveness, then eat everything in sight. Drink all the wine in those tiny goblets, too." Poor city-slum children were the invisible hungry ghosts, living spirits that the rest of society had abandoned.

My mother didn't practice traditional rituals or partake in worship because she had a modern education. She sneered at religious practice, calling it superstition. I became more curious; nothing was taken for granted. I took in everything as if I were a living camera recording the sense, color, and texture of things. Every day a fascinating world presented me with its best candid shots. These amazing recollections help me now with my writing, but at the time I felt strange, a child not at home in her own world.

When I was eight we moved to Taiwan. In the early Fifties, Taipei was still a small city surrounded by farming communities. Lush rice paddies, ox-drawn carts, farmers fishing for eels in the river, women beating laundry on the flat rocks along the river bed, dragonflies, trees laden with papayas, olives, mangoes, figs—a paradise welcomed me. I roamed the whole countryside, climbing tall olive trees, digging soft clay and wild edible roots, picking wild berries, soaking my feet in puddles, praising the earth with my whole being. The dead spirit in me was resurrected as I bathed in summer showers and counted magic clouds. The heavenly animal parade of the sunset asked me to join them.

I spent most of my spare time exploring the wilderness. On lazy afternoons everyone napped or took refuge in the shade. The bits and pieces of cement scattered around our neighborhood were hot enough to grill food. Even cats and dogs hid. I went alone to explore the ruins of an old mud temple, an abandoned well, a burial ground for animals, a path of wildflowers, a hidden stream that ran through a wooded area, a rice-threshing ground, a special wet shallow near the river filled with soft white clay, the tallest olive tree in the vicinity. Ignorance of the native dialect, even a brush with the law, when a cop chased me out of a private property, didn't discourage me; a warrior's spirit was with me then. The daring exploration of those years provided me with vision, courage, direct connection to the earth and sky. I remember sitting outside in an afternoon of pouring rain, feeling the cool wetness penetrating the pores of my skin, listening to its sound washing over me. Then a rainbow and a magnificent tropical sunset embraced me, uplifting me, offering a fantastic ode to life.

In school I had a great painting teacher, Mr. Ho. He was quite young, but his wisdom was wild and unlike that of other teachers, who were strict and authoritarian. Mr. Ho taught us to create painting the way we explored our world, to fill our sheets of big paper with sights, sounds, smells, and actions of the marketplace and the green countryside, ripe fruit trees, the street performer directing his monkeys, the popcorn man with his cast-iron popper, the rag collector, the melon man, the won-ton man beating his bamboo clappers, women washing clothes by the river bank, kids tending their ducks, water-buffalo. My world transformed under Mr. Ho's guidance. I painted in an intense manner like Van Gogh; the other children in my school didn't paint like that. Years later in college, when I learned about the great Dutch painter, I found a kindred spirit. Van Gogh immersed himself in nature, in the dance of sun, letting himself be possessed by the spirit of light. He was also a stranger on earth whom others didn't understand or accept. I found a thread in his life that connected with my own. The sufferings of the world threatened to overwhelm us, yet there was a part of our souls that wanted to dance with light. Painting became a new language, a healing language.

A Secret Lotus Garden

A scent guides me. I enter
by crawling under the brambles.
A dark green world opens before me: giant green pods
float upon a pond, cradles holding dews and frogs;
a willow tree drops its leafy hair over the water;
white buds of lotus dance high above the murky
green; croaks of frogs, drones of insects.
A stillness holds everything.
A deep green world made brilliant
by a sudden flash of white light.
My tongue sweetened by scent of lotus, I put my palms
together and praise. It's a wonder that a lotus rises
out of mud yet does not give out its stench.

In a secret garden of lotus, a wild mind
is opening, rising out of the dark, murky green.

During my elementary school years I was a poor student; teachers wrote in my report cards that I didn't pay attention in the class and spent all the days dreaming. There were two subjects in which I did excel: music and art. My gift for singing taught me to treasure words and eventually led me to narrative poetry, in operatic form. I remember hearing street peddlers singing, fortune tellers belting out chants in markets, and sometimes, on a small, makeshift stage, local opera singers rendering their own version of the classic "The Monkey King." Through opera I discovered words had shapes, textures, and an authority of their own. When I ventured to a section of Hong Kong called Old Hong Kong recently, I found an enthusiastic crowd enjoying the opera.

My fondest memory of my childhood is of those moments when I performed in front of people. Sharing my talent garnered me a kind of nurture, the approval and praise I craved. And in the heart of praise there was a song. I was seven years old, standing on a red velvet-draped stage, embraced by shimmery threads of light. I stared into a dark auditorium filled with beckoning breaths; I found a huge magnetic field that could charge each cell within me. Wearing a blue satin gown, I was an angel. Each vibrato touched the dome. Six hundred pairs of hands applauded my long-held note, followed by a melody that brought the house down. And I was soaring.

My mother had tried unsuccessfully many ways to immigrate to America. In her own account, she was a journalist dispatched to Spain. I thought moving to Madrid from Taiwan was my mother's inventive way to get to America. Back in the Fifties, Asians were not allowed to immigrate to the States.

Once we settled in Madrid, my mother decided to tutor us in Chinese. She ordered a whole set of books from Taipei and taught me how to read, making me appreciate the beauty of Chu Yuen, Li Po, Tu Fu, Su Tung Po, Po Chu I and other ancient Chinese poets. I came to revel in words. A thousand years of Chinese bones could be found in few chosen words of master poets. From Tu Fu's "The Journey North: The Homecoming" (translated by Arthur Cooper):

> Slowly, slowly we tramped country tracks,
> With cottage smoke rarely on their winds;
> Of those we met, many suffered wounds
> Still oozing blood, and they moaned aloud!

A few stanzas further he described the pain experienced by fugitives of warring times:

> I had fallen, too, in Tartar dust
> But can return with my hair like flour,
> A year but past, to my simple home
> And my own wife, in a hundred rags;

Who sees me, cries like the wind through trees,
Weeps like the well sobbing underground;
And then my son, pride of all my days,
With his face, too, whiter than the snows.

We had few material possessions beside books. Through literature I took flight to different worlds—Chinese translations of Russian novels, American novels, French writers. Years later, I also discovered in the library the plays of Garcia Lorca, Tennessee Williams, Chekhov, poetry of St. John of the Cross, Pablo Neruda, Walt Whitman, Thoreau, works that lifted me out of gloom. With the words of masters I started to build myself, strengthening my bones, so I could dance to their music and meditation. When I wasn't reading I drew pictures, copied old post cards and café scenes, flowers, butterflies, from restaurant menus.

My teen years were torn by sexual awakenings and assaults. No one taught me about lust, desires; those were things I saw in Hollywood movies, in the body of Marilyn Monroe, the face of Greta Garbo, the seductive movements of Sophia Loren, the lusty looks of Brigitte Bardot. But I was a tall, skinny Chinese girl, suddenly landed in Spain. For over a year I studied in a convent, where the teenage girls showed me photos of their idols in their wallets—all had the same guy with a big, greased hairdo and slick smile. Much later I learned those were pictures of Elvis—that was how innocent and ignorant I was. Boys and old men smacked their wet hungry lips onto mine whenever they could catch me alone. Stealing a kiss from a *chinita* was a special triumph. I didn't like their slimy tongues or their panting breaths. Once this pudgy guy, a student in a tutorial school I went to for a year, chased me all over the school, begging me to be his wife. I was so frightened I climbed up to the top of a grape arbor and stayed there until he left.

My first menstrual period led me to experience the passion of Spanish people, a great contrast to the reserved manners of the Chinese. For weeks I felt my body change, my breasts grow soft to the touch. One morning the landlady found my blood-stained underwear soaking in the bidet. That afternoon when I returned from the market, she had gathered a small crowd in the living room. The men clapped their hands and stomped their heels on the floor, one of them belting out Andalusian gypsy melodies like cries of the soul, while another played Flamenco guitar. "Heh, Chinita, ahora tu es una mujer, una mujer!" the crowd cheered and applauded my entrance. Cigarette smoke fogged the features of people around me, but I could see tears streaming down my landlady's cheeks. Suddenly I felt my nipples stiffen; the men in the room had peeled off my clothes with their stares. The women, moving their hips sensually, laughed with gusto at my awkwardness. Someone offered me a full glass of red wine. I stared into the cup and felt nauseated, but I drank it, savoring the bittersweetness of womanhood. The next morning I discovered I had passed out from one glass of wine.

In the morning I went to get a loaf of fresh *pan* and olives; the smell of *pan* and olives, *paella* cooking on a wood stove, *churros*, and other sights and tastes still bring back my days in Spain. But there were also days of hunger, of waiting in long lines to buy potatoes, or eating sour soups and moldy cheese from the church's soup kitchen. Hunger eventually drove my mother to leave Spain. By then she had given birth to another boy. My mother took off to America, searching for jobs and a place for her family. I was twelve, left in Madrid for over six months by myself to care for my three younger brothers. I grew up fast in hard times. My mother's letters from New York informed me that we would never go hungry in America. We would have a chicken in our pot every day, and clothes and toys were plentiful, cheap at the Woolworth. The early Chinese immigrants had rightfully called America "Goldmountain."

Minutes before landing, I caught a glimpse of the Statue of Liberty; a Goddess of Democracy guarded the entrance to this great country. I arrived in New York City when I was thirteen, in 1960. I was still a mute, except when I sang. Inside my heart I carried stories that I would discover and set free when I grew older. Our luggage consisted mainly of books and one huge basket of Chinese cooking utensils—a wok, a rice-cooking pot, a tea kettle, a chopping block, chopsticks, bowls, and cups. The customs officer didn't even inspect each item; he sniffed at our bags and baskets and dismissed us. Riding through the city to the Lower East Side, I was overwhelmed by the tall, concrete structures. A tree-less world. How could I survive? We moved into a tenement in Little Italy, surrounded by other tenements. The windows of our three-room apartment looked out into a factory and a small, dirty, concrete courtyard. I remember the siren calls from the factory at noon, the sight of huge dead rats in the coldest days of winter, the banging of the radiators, and the hissing of pipes that woke me from my dreams. Even the few hours when the sun shone in on our place each day seemed sinister. I felt cheated by my dream of America. The Goldmountain was devoid of the tree-lined avenues and majestic fountains of Madrid. My mother was suffering the hard life of a lone pioneer. She held many jobs, working in an all-night coffee shop, in a factory, cleaning the Chinese theatre in Chinatown. For months my mother threw countless crying fits while washing laundry in a tub in the middle of our kitchen-living room. After school we did bead work at home. Through my aunt in Hong Kong, every month my mother sent money to my sisters and grandmother in mainland China.

I thought this time I would truly die. Joining my ancestors was better than struggling in a barren city where we had no relatives or friends, nor a good command of the language. The nightmares of my earliest childhood returned. I had feverish days when I had to stay home alone, listening to the sound of the factory and the meek longings of my own heart, and I had recurring dreams about being caught in a huge net; no matter how I struggled I could not get free.

English was like sawdust in my mouth, the words choked me. Its grammar and pronunciation were so difficult, its idioms impossible for a newcomer to master. I always carried a small pocket English-Chinese dictionary; in a few years I wore out half a dozen of them. But there were so many words that I couldn't find in my little book, like *wise guy, loony bin, fucked-up, groovy*. I missed Spanish, the precision of its pronunciation, its grammatical structure, and its special musical quality. A language I had come to trust and love was now useless. English had one purpose then; people spat it at me. "Go back to where you came from, Chink, Gook, Slanty Eyes, Yellow Face." I felt angry, ugly, and helpless. Even the Chinese kids didn't speak my dialect; they spoke Toisanese and I spoke Mandarin. Again I became absorbed in drawing, in a world where language had no purpose.

In Seward Park High School I was still shy, but some kids liked and befriended me. Petra, the tallest girl in the whole school, took me to Henry Street Settlement, a bustling art community. There I did ceramic sculpture, sang in the chorus, watched dancers rehearse. The first time Petra took me to hear Bach, it was the "St. Matthew Passion," before Easter, at the Riverside Church. I remember being moved to tears, uplifted by words whose specific meanings I didn't know. The voices of the double chorus soothed me like medicine. Music partially relieved the rage and anguish in me; I began to find my ability to love. Later another friend, George, took me to hear Thelonious Monk at the Village Vanguard. We didn't have money for tickets, and there was a crowd that night. We waited outside until after hours. Around one in the morning we sneaked in and heard a big man call to us, "Hey, boy and girl, come in, come right in." I remember his wide smile, his fingers dancing across the keys, his zest for life. In the sound of jazz I rediscovered my own ability to improvise, my craving for spontaneity. I secretly laughed, glad that I had not forgotten how to play.

In the days of the Vietnam War, Washington Square was rife with hippies, druggies, folk musicians, and older men, all experienced in grabbing young girls with their hands, their hungry stares. I—a wide-eyed child, nicknamed "Miss Shanghai"—along with my Japanese girlfriend, got invited to an old Italian singer's studio. In the midst of singing Italian arias the guy suddenly stopped, grabbed me in his arms, and forced a kiss on me while squeezing my breasts. My friend and I managed to escape by pushing our way out of the singer's place and running as fast as our legs could go. Another incident bore the same kind of evil: a painter slipped me a drink laced with LSD. The hallucinatory experience had no ill effect, but that man's sneaky act made me mistrust other men.

Those were years of war against bodies, souls, against the people of Vietnam. I saw my friends destroyed by drugs, volatile relationships, and a philosophy of "there's no tomorrow." A popular girl, a friend in school, killed herself; a soprano in the chorus had an illegal abortion; another classmate overdosed with heroin and died. Were they Flower Children? Privileged middle-class whites playing with fire? I thought I was a member of the Lost Generation. I had journeyed through Dante's Hell and—like a Vietnam vet—I still carry scars and burn marks from those years. Even the inspirational music of Dylan and Baez could not resurrect the part of me that died as I came to the realization that the middle class and the working class would never be able to come to a resolution in values and personal conduct or to acknowledge the gap between haves and have-nots. I was a poor girl with homemade clothes, hanging out with kids who romanticized slumming in the ghetto and flaunted their anti-conformity with ragged clothes and messy hair.

With the Bread and Puppet Theatre, I joined the first peace marchers down Fifth Avenue, holding a large Uncle Sam puppet that looked exactly like LBJ. Bikers tried to break up our procession, throwing red paint on the marchers. Some tried to attack me, the only Asian face in the front line. "Mistress of Mao, how much you're getting paid to march here, from Peking?" How ironic those words sounded in my ears. My father had been killed because he was accused of being anti-Communist.

I entered City College concentrating on sculpture, painting, and drawing. Stories were still buried deep inside of me. Art provided a community that kept me safe.

AURA LUZ SANCHEZ

WHEN DUSK DESCENDS

I. The Injury

On a drowsy day when time danced
a waltz in the weary arms
of August summer
and overheated blossoms drooped
like bowed heads at Sunday Mass
a phone rang,
a voice announced the news
of the injury.

Now, like stale air,
I linger by your bedside;
you lie there limp inside your limbs.
Our thoughts, continents once connected,
share a past of prolific moments
petrified by our stone existence,
waiting for new shoots to grow.

II. *What's His Name?*

                       she asks me.
Does he have his clinic card?
I stiffen, sensing your contours fading
to the sepia of an antique photo.
Last week the waitress at The Landing
asked me for your order.

As if it's not enough—
your body—
two years ago
strong as the pumpkin pine
driftwood on our shore,
transformed by you
into our dining table,
energetic as the power tools
you deftly used to make our
picture frames.

Independent, you survived
the Maine woods with only Calamus,
your dog, for company.
You've become a third world country,
stripped of resources,
dependent on the first world
for the very crops you used to grow
abundantly.

Your professorial robes once
swishing down the aisles of Pomp and Circumstance
are now pinned silent
like the prim bun of a cloistered nun.
Ironic
that the fast-paced
squash you loved to play
would stun you into stillness.

Like the father denounced
by the Chinese son
you're ordered under house arrest.
Nerves once a part of a well-planned scheme
taunt you falsely,
careen like bumper cars,
inflict random pain,
thoughtlessly inviting arctic and equatorial demons
to possess you.

Yet the whitewater swiftness of your mind,
becoming your protector,
escapes the sentence.
My name is Frank, you bellow
and roll your chair away.

III. When Dusk Descends

Relentless quills pierce
with menace,
deflate our spirits,
cast our hopes up against rocks
hidden by an inundating tide.
Like appalled disciples

damning their guru for having sinned,
we curse a life which
once was secure
like cotton candy on its cone,
swaddled
in the soft of eiderdown.

Splashes of salty freedom
only memory now,
boating to the harbor islands,
riding converging crests
of churning waves
like cowboys at a rodeo,
lying snug in our sleeping bags
in the sanctuaries
of New England forests. At dawn
the woods filled with wafts
of iron-skillet bacon and brewed
coffee from the Andes.

Holidays, once in high relief,
are sepia images of a past.
A panoply of pain consumes us.
And yet, when dusk descends
and we sit for supper,
we still make plans
to greet the sacred daybreak
of tomorrow.

LI MIN MO

DAWN SPITS OUT WILD HORSES

She gets out of work at the cusp
of day, feels the steam from
the manhole on Delancey wrapping
around her like ancient spirits.

It seems so long ago when
mountains and rivers were spirits
that danced through me and the rain
purified my body that labored under the sun.

She heads east, strolling across Norfolk,
noticing the ginkgo leaves fanned like
children's faces in half-light.

Life-lines are just stories, that was
what my great-grandmother told me.

The sun in a rapture, pink kisses
waltz in the sky, dawn spits out wild
horses across the East River.

My palms used to hold a story. I knew
how to praise the earth with open-throated
songs, elongated notes that brought
the sky close to my heart.

She starts to race, taking in the cold,
pain in her heels, tightness in her chest.
Sweat like bitter medicine cleanses
her waitress night.

There used to be a horse running
wild through the center of my life,
wearing no blinders, her hooves
sinking into beds of wildflowers,

nostrils flaring with summer heat,
every part of her ready
to spring and canter to the song:
"Take me, sky, take me all."

Purple sky beasts merge with flames
of red, rose melts into gold, silver
of daylight; they tango across
the eastern sky, then disappear
into the mouth of sea.

When she slows down on Elizabeth
Street, she hears bells ringing. A tired
nag the color of clouds pulls a cart
full of fresh fruit, its wheels squeaking
a sad chant. The seller with a tattered
brown felt hat nods to her. She buys
a pound of Delicious apples, offers one
to the mare, and whispers,

Do you know?

ELENA HARAP

CILLA'S SPACE

in memory of Cilla Gibbs

In Cilla's space
Spanish señoritas in red lace gowns teach tap dance steps
to men in bowler hats

in Cilla's space
there is a magic, bottomless cup of tea

in Cilla's space
long-lost sisters recognize each other
by the dust-mote secrets in their eyes

in Cilla's space
bosomy Victorian dress forms hark to trolleys' music,
flounce their flowered skirts
and go out for a walk down Centre Street

followed by the lacy señoritas
followed by the men in bowler hats
followed by the long-lost sisters

followed by a little girl in purple overalls
and a second little girl, holding by the hand
a tall trombone player on roller skates!

Cilla smiles,
she lets them go;
she says: *Now I've got some space!*

MARY MILLNER McCULLOUGH

CALLIE

Callie climbed the cement steps to her favorite perch at the edge of the front porch. Like a cool iron on a hot stove, her feet felt the heat enter through their soles. She pulled back into the shade. These were the dog days of August. Callie knew the heat made dogs go mad. Her small frame remained alert, just in case some wild dog should stray into her yard. Mr. Washington sometimes let hunting dogs roam free to chase children. She had seen him peering out, from behind his curtains, as she ran past his house, hoping not to be noticed by him or his dogs.

Callie lived at the eastern end of Roundpipe, a small factory town, on the corner of Beth and Will Streets. Her Aunt Frannie lived three yards away. Callie had come home after being left with her Aunt Frannie while her pa went to work at the furniture factory. Aunt Frannie stayed home to take care of her sisters' children while the sisters went to take care of white ladies' children for money, hand-me-downs, and leftovers. Callie's ma was still in the special hospital her pa had taken her to after the baby was born. The baby was almost a year old now. Callie tried not to think about how long Ma had been gone. Her aunt, too busy washing clothes and yelling at all the children she watched, did not see Callie leave the yard. Her cousin Deedee, playing near the fence that enclosed the yard, had seen Callie lift the latch on the gate and slip away. Callie knew Deedee would not tell, in exchange for some favor later.

Miss Rosie, on her way to work, spoke to the thin, gold-colored girl. "How's your ma, Callie?" Miss Rosie inquired from the road.

"Pa say she better," replied Callie.

"She be home soon then," said the woman. Her words echoed through the empty house beyond the porch and came back to Callie through the walls. Callie, in her faded feed-sack dress that had fit well last summer when her ma made it, watched the woman walk on and disappear over the hill.

Callie's grandparents lived at the end of the pavement on

Will Street. Beyond their house, Will Street became a dirt road and adventures began. If Callie stayed in the front of her house or just played on the sunny side near the lilac bushes, her grandparents wouldn't see her. About ten in the morning she knew her grandma would come out of her house to sit on the front porch in her favorite rocking chair, and a few minutes later Grandpa would arrive to sit in his swing. They would spend their day rocking and swinging. Grandpa was a Baptist preacher without a church and a farmer who never owned a farm. He had quit being a sharecropper to grow watermelons and vegetables on the hill behind his house. His specialties were the Bible and "ash" potatoes. It was years before Callie knew he meant Irish potatoes.

In Roundpipe almost all the people were related to each other. Many of the wood frame houses were home to Callie's aunts and first, second, and third cousins. Callie had been taught that it was important to know all her blood cousins. From what she overheard in her aunts' kitchens, she guessed that she needed this information so she wouldn't end up married to one of her boy cousins. Callie had overheard her aunts laughing in the kitchen about men who couldn't stop themselves from marrying their cousins. They talked about Mr. String, who married his first cousin and had children who never grew up. Callie's mother said that in his case it was his wife who couldn't help herself. "That's why her children are so mismatched, all shapes and colors," her ma said.

Aunt Frannie noticed Callie lingering outside the screen door and said, "Little pitchers have big ears." Callie had run off to play that day before her ma's familiar words could reach her ears. Sitting on the porch saying, "Go play, Callie," over and over to herself, she tried to find the sound of her ma.

Callie found out about grown-ups' secrets from standing outside screen doors. Listening was the easy part. Figuring out what some of the things she heard meant was more difficult. She knew about the white man who came twice a week into Roundpipe, driving his black model-T Ford down Beth Street and up Will Street. Callie had seen him from her perch at the top of the steps. Once she had run through the house into the back yard and let her eyes follow his car as it disappeared down the ungraveled, rutted road that went past her grandpa's house. That road, filled with deep gullies created by summer rainstorms, was dangerous. She had seen the man twice a week all summer. He went into the woods where escaped convicts from prison farms hid. Callie wondered if he would find the path that led to Miss Emmie's house. That house was hard to find. You had to know which direction to take, once the road ended.

Miss Emmie lived there with Mr. Jacks. Miss Emmie and Callie's ma were friends. She had heard them talking many times. Callie didn't like Miss Emmie because she was always asking Callie's ma, "Has Callie done this? Has Callie done that?" That nosy Miss Emmie even asked, in front of Callie, if she had started her monthly. "I started when I was eight years old," Miss Emmie told Ma.

At the moment of that question, Callie felt the same disgust for Miss Emmie that her grandma had often expressed. "Lily, how can you let that woman in your house; she's so black," Callie overheard her say to her ma.

"Like the black coal that I burn to keep my house warm, Miss Emmie fuels my heart. She is one of God's creatures and my friend," Callie's ma answered. Callie never heard her grandma say anything about Miss Emmie to her ma again. She did say things to Callie about Miss Emmie when Ma wasn't around to hear. Callie knew that her grandpa and her ma studied the Bible, looking for guidance in how people should be treated. While Grandpa and Ma believed in doing unto others as you would have them do unto you, her grandma always said, "Do unto others before they do unto you."

Callie remembered the first time her ma had taken her along on one of her visits to Miss Emmie's house. They walked down Will Street until it turned into a narrow path that led into the woods. Shafts of sunlight bounced off dogwood trees. Songs of hidden birds accompanied honeysuckle smells. She forgot to fear escaped convicts. She could see mountains in the distance as she and her mother descended into a little valley. Roundpipe Hill was much steeper than she had imagined. It was a glorious adventure. She trailed behind and sometimes ran ahead, but never so far out of sight that she couldn't look back to see her mother.

The house appeared so abruptly in a clearing at the edge of the path that it made Callie feel as if she had entered Miss Emmie's home without knocking. Trees and bushes barely tolerated its presence. Callie stood looking at the brightly painted yellow wooden frame house as she waited for her ma to catch up to her. Callie had never seen a yellow house. Wood houses were faded white or gray. The white lady her ma worked for lived in a red brick house. Miss Emmie's house sat on the ground like a pumpkin in a patch. The front porch running the full length of the house appeared as flat as the paper dolls she made from the Sears and Roebuck catalogue everyone called the "wish" book. Everything except the woman bent over in the yard was all angles, lines, and points. There were no curves, no rises, no hills to climb or descend, just a bright house daring her to think it was not a proper house. As Miss Emmie stood up, her flowered house dress opened, exposing black breasts as shocking to Callie as the yellow house. Lowering her eyes from Miss Emmie's shame, Callie saw boots like the ones her pa wore when he walked in snake grass. Of course, he always had laces holding the boot tongue inside. The tongues of Miss Emmie's boots were saying hello to the big toe protruding through the top of the boot. Single droplets of sweat took turns leaving Miss Emmie's face. Callie stood still, wishing she could catch them before they broke into pieces on the ground.

"How y'all doing today, Lily? Come in and sit a spell," Miss Emmie had invited Callie and her ma.

"Go play, Callie," was her ma's way of accepting the invitation.

Callie pretended to go to the back yard but turned back at the corner of the porch. She stood still, out of sight, to listen to her ma and Miss Emmie talk. She heard Ma say, "There are days when I wished for no more than that Pete would not come home for lunch. I've made three meals a day for ten years."

"I know what you mean. Up, make breakfast, lunch, and cook supper. At least you have Callie to help you. Can she make the bread for you?" asked Miss Emmie.

"She's learning, but I can't trust her to do it by herself yet. She doesn't pay no attention to what she's doing . . . . I thought Mr. Jacks took his lunch with him. Why do you have to make a lunch?" her ma asked.

"You know I have to cook for Mr. Les twice a week. He likes to come here for his lunch since his wife died. I get to make a little money for my rainy day."

"Emmie, you told me that Mr. Jacks didn't want you to work for that man in his house. Why he let you cook his lunch for him at your house?" her ma had asked.

"He don't know," replied Miss Emmie.

"What if he finds out?" Lily asked. "Mr. Jacks is going to be mad you are doing what he done ask you not to do."

"He won't find out. Mr. Les comes for lunch and Mr. Jacks comes for dinner," Miss Emmie said. And they both laughed.

"I don't know how you do it, taking care of two men, and keeping them straight in their coming and going," Lily said.

"T'aint hard. They want the same thing, full bellies and a ready and willing woman. If I can get a little something I want from them, I'm happy," Miss Emmie replied.

Lily, looking out into the woods beyond, said, "Rev. Harris says one of the Ten Commandments tells us not to commit adultery."

"Don't apply to me. We common-law man and wife, just live together, ain't got married in no church. And besides, that reverend of yours don't seem to follow his own preaching."

"What do you mean by that?" asked Lily.

"Last Saturday night, Mr. Jacks and me saw your preacher coming out of the Dew Drop Inn with his choir director," said Miss Emmie.

"She works there. He probably was picking her up for choir practice," Lily retorted.

"You have choir practice at midnight these days," was all Miss Emmie said.

"Callie, come on," her mother had called without moving from her seat. "Time to go home. Come have some sassafras tea with me tomorrow, Miss Emmie."

"Before lunch or before supper?" Miss Emmie asked.

"Suit yourself," Lily answered. Sensing that her ma was ending the visit, Callie ran up, pretending to be out of breath.

The best part of that day had been walking on the path with her ma. On the way home Callie ran ahead, beating at the bushes, giving notice to snakes to take a detour. She waited for her ma to catch up before asking, "Ma, who is Mr. Les?"

"Callie, how many times have I told you not to listen to grown-ups talk. You just put what you heard out of your head," her ma said. They ended their walk in silence. Callie thought she knew all the colored men who lived near them. Mr. Les must live on the west end of town where the better-off colored families lived. Whoever he was, her ma thought Miss Emmie was breaking the adult-tree commandment with him.

The sun forced Callie to leave her dreaming and the porch. She wandered to the vegetable garden behind the house. Walking between the rows of tomatoes, squash, and cucumbers, she counted each row, keeping in her mind a combination of even and odd numbers. She played a game, pointing to the vegetables while she sang a rhyme in her private language. The magic number for Callie was five. At the fifth row, making sure there were no green horned worms on the plant's stem, she picked a tomato. "You're gonna be snake-bit before summer's out, if you don't wear your shoes, Callie," she said, trying to mimic her ma's voice.

Callie carried the warm tomato into the kitchen, peeled the skin, and sliced the tomato onto a saucer. She took some store-bought bread from the bread box and some of her ma's made-up salad dressing from the icebox. The cucumber from the table on the back porch was the last of the bunch she had picked for her ma. Callie spread big spoonfuls of salad dressing on each slice of bread after she had removed the crust. She added all the slices of tomato and cucumber that would fit on the bread, and ate the leftover pieces. She poured cold sweet milk made from canned evaporated milk, water, and sugar, into a glass jar and took the lunch to her perch at the edge of the front porch. Callie put the milk down on the porch beside her and placed the saucer with the sandwich on her lap. She waited.

The twelve o'clock whistle blew at the furniture factory. Time for lunch. She reached for her sandwich. Callie saw the white man driving the black model-T Ford turn onto Will Street. She put her sandwich down and ran to the bicycle she had left leaning against the smokehouse. She rode out of her yard onto Will Street, following the black car. Grandpa and Grandma sat watching her ride toward them. As usual, Grandma was as far away from Grandpa as she could get and still be on the porch.

"Cal-LEE, where are you going?" Grandma called to her. Callie made a slow and reluctant circle in front of their house.

"Just riding my bike, Grandma."

"Nealie, it's too hot for that child to be moving about," her grandpa said.

Callie headed back to her yard. She was not allowed to go beyond their house. Riding a cousin on her handlebars, she could sometimes get away with going further down Will Street as long as she did not get out of their eyesight. With two people on the bike she could pretend that she couldn't stop right away. She knew that they enjoyed her game, waiting to see how long she could keep the bike upright with two people on it. Callie didn't know who made the distance rule or what might happen if she broke it. She just never went any further when the sentinels were on duty.

Parking her bike against the smokehouse, Callie walked through the silence of the house towards her abandoned lunch. She stood in the coolness of the room before reaching out to open the door to the front porch. Her mouth fell open, as if she were a baby bird waiting to be fed its first worm. Sucked-in air dried the roof of her mouth as she tried to pull light into all the corners of the room. Her eyes carried her to the unfinished dress her ma had left in her sewing basket. The pieces, placed one on top of the other, had the cut-out newspaper pattern still attached. Callie had napped in this room on summer days while her ma made winter dresses. Taking a thin quilt from the back of the couch, Callie folded it, formed a pallet on the floor, and lay down as if to take a nap.

She remembered her protests at taking naps from summers before. Callie did not like the idea of resting in the afternoon on hot days. Rest for Callie meant sleep. Sleep meant that she ceased to exist. This afternoon, the heat threatened to imprison her on her quilt pallet and pushed her into the floor, into oblivion. No air stirred.

Callie felt like a stranger in her own house. She could see the spot where the coal stove had been moved out for the summer, the green couch against the windows that faced Mrs. Martin's house, and the door that led to the pantry where canned peaches, beans, and tomatoes were stored for the winter meals. Through the door she could see the red and white enamel kitchen table and the wood-burning cook stove. The cook stove would be lit by Callie at three-thirty. She would reheat the beans her ma had cooked. She would add tomatoes with sugar sprinkled over them. It was her favorite meal.

Restless and no longer interested in eating, Callie got up from the floor before the house caught her in its sad embrace. Leaving by way of the enclosed back porch, Callie glanced at the old ice box and the empty table where her ma kept vegetables picked for canning. She held the screen door so that it would not bang; she left the house's echoes behind her. Jumping over the hot cement walk onto warm clover grass, she watched the bees fly away from her toes. The grass felt comfortable and safe. Bees sting, she had been told. She had accidentally stepped on a bee once and it had stung her. She decided that if she didn't step on them, they wouldn't sting her.

Callie was proud of the yard that surrounded her house. There was the formal front yard where no one was allowed to play on the grass. The grass was surrounded by a hedge her pa constantly cut and trimmed. The front yard was for the neighbors and passersby. The spaces on each side of the house were very different. The part of the yard that bordered on Will Street was dark and damp. It was the area where Callie could hear convicts' chains clang against the ground. Searching for a lost ball one evening before dark, she saw Mr. Singer carry his daughter home to die. Callie could never catch the sun in that yard.

The opposite was true on the other side of the house. Flowers grew well there. Birds visited, bees lived among the blooming clover, and every once in a while a snake would meander through. The flowering bushes attracted robins, redbirds, and bluebirds.

From where she stood, Callie could see the two fruit trees her parents planted before they had her, the small blue and green grape arbor, the cherry tree that fed the birds, and the lone yellow apple tree. Sitting on the round metal cap that covered the water meter was a big, fat robin. Maybe this time she could capture herself a bird. All she needed was salt for its tail. She turned, ran quickly and quietly in and out of the still house. Bending from her waist into a crouching position, Callie prepared her body for the hunt. Carrying salt in the palm of her right hand, she became invisible to all robins and hoped that she could stay that way until the hunt came to a successful end. Inching towards the bird with her right hand stretched out before her, she held her breath. There was no outburst from the three crows on a nearby fence, and the cries of buzzards circling in the distance did not reach the robin's ears. There were no sounds from her cousins on the other side of Will Street. There were no words of inquiry from Mrs. Martin, who had no children, only two grown-up drunks for sons. No one said, "Leave that bird alone." She traveled on the light from the afternoon sun.

Callie's tongue pushed through her mouth and ran over her lips. Hairs stood at attention on her body. This fat robin would not leave her today. Callie's right hand arrived at the robin's tail. Losing the larger wet chunk to the ground, she sent two fingers and a thumb forward from her clenched fist to place a pinch of salt on the robin's tail. She moved her left hand into position to be ready to catch the robin when it fell over in a daze from the salt on its tail. She closed her eyes in raptured anticipation, imagining the feel of its feathers, its warmth in her hand and its heart beating against the palm of her left hand.

She cried out, "I have it! I have it!"

Opening her eyes, Callie did not see a robin in her left hand. When she looked at her right hand, she saw moist crystals of salt shining between her fingers like diamonds. The hunt was over. Callie emerged from invisibility arm by arm.

She heard a faint "Callie, Callie." The cry sounded like Aunt Frannie calling her from a faraway place. The buzzards circled closer. The robin was nowhere to be seen.

Callie followed the crows' cawing to the front yard and climbed the hot steps. Black ants had covered her sandwich, and their extended family had formed a line that descended into the sweet milk. Callie watched them while she thought about the man in the black car. Where did he go? Wherever it was, he went there twice a week. She knew he could go only so far on the road before he would have to get out of the car and walk on the path that would take him to Miss Emmie's house. Why? Was he a salesman? Why didn't he stop at other houses? What could he be selling that only she bought? Chickens or chicken feed? She did raise chickens in her yard. As Callie sat asking and answering her own questions, a factory whistle signaled that the lunch hour was over. The black car with the white man in it came down Will Street and turned up Beth Lane just as her Aunt Frannie came down the road. The car slowed and the white man tipped his hat to her aunt as she walked by.

"Callie, didn't you hear me calling you?" her aunt demanded.

Staring at the car leaving Roundpipe, Callie asked her aunt, "Who that white man?"

"That's Mr. Les. He owns the store at the end of the road," replied her aunt.

"Is that the man Miss Emmie makes lunch for twice a week?" asked Callie.

"Where'd you hear that?" her aunt asked. And before Callie could answer she said, "Miss Emmie don't cook for that white man." Her aunt spat the words at her as if they might turn sour in her mouth if they stayed near her tongue too long. Callie knew she could add another grown-up secret to the others she had collected. The answer to her question came in the way the words came out hot and stinging through Aunt Frannie's lips.

Callie savored her new knowledge. Miss Emmie entertained a white man in her house for lunch twice a week to make money for her rainy day. She did so even after Mr. Jacks had told her not to do it. That must be what it meant to commit adultery.

Callie could hear the thunder in the distance announcing the storm headed for Roundpipe later in the afternoon. The cooler air arriving before the storm made her shiver. "Feels like someone's walking on my grave," said Aunt Frannie as they left Callie's house behind.

The next whistle would blow at four o'clock. At exactly four-ten, from her aunt's porch Callie would see Mr. Jacks, in his black model-T Ford, travel down Beth Lane, turn onto Will Street, and go past her grandpa's house onto the rutted road. He would leave his car to walk on the narrow path to the flat house that sprang up so abruptly in the woods. Miss Emmie would be there, willing and ready, to give him his supper.

BLANCA BONILLA

FEBRUARY SEVENTEENTH

It's Saturday, cold and sunny. I am lying in my bed, looking through the window, listening to the wind blowing outside. Through the cracks of the old windows strange sounds trespass. I get chills with the thought of being outside. Over the past two weeks the temperature has dropped to zero degrees. My mother walks into the room to let me know that it's ten o'clock. As I am getting out of bed I feel wet. "My period . . . not today . . . shit." I walk towards the mirror to see the new color of my hair; from a redhead I have become a brunette in just a matter of hours! I look at two big pimples on my face. I am really feeling ugly.

I go through the day, stressed, anxious, nervous, and overwhelmed by the tasks I have to take care of, but at the same time I feel happy. I keep asking myself, "Why do I want to go through so much pressure for just one day?" Time is flying by; it's already three-thirty and I need to be ready by four-thirty. I place my gown on the bed and my makeup on the dresser. I take a good look at the bedroom I love so much, where I always feel comfortable. I have been in this room for a number of years, and I won't be here tomorrow. Now I am sad; transitions are not easy for me.

My mother walks in with Ms. Torres, my high school teacher. She hugs me and smiles. "I am sorry to come early, but I have a commitment later on. I wanted to come and help you get ready." She starts putting on my makeup. I close my eyes as she works on my face. "Blanca, you are only seventeen. Why?" Nothing comes out of my mouth, although I feel uncomfortable at having someone question my decision. I open my eyes and approve of what I see. My face looks good, therefore I feel better. I stand up and start putting on my gown. My teacher looks at me with admiration and warmth as she helps me put on my veil. "You make a beautiful bride." She hugs me and leaves. I look around my bedroom, breathe deeply in and out as I open the door to continue my journey.

RAMÓN

Su mirada tímida de inseguridad
penetró en mi corazón
como llama ardiente
de lo que llamamos amor.

Con su pelo negro rizado
sus ojos oscuros azabache
su sonrisa sin malicias
y con sus buenos modales—

"Un hombre bueno," dijo mi padre,
"pues le gusta trabajar
mejorar su futuro
y mantener un hogar."

Mi madre dijo, "Es buen mozo,
y buenos sentimientos trae él;
pues hay que darle el discurso
y la entrada sin temer."

Tres días a la semana
me visitaba sin fallar
con supervisión de mis padres—
el tiempo lo hizo pensar.

Me ofreció matrimonio
y por la boda pagó.
Nos unimos como pareja
y así fue que comenzó.

Seis meses después
preñada me encontré yo
llena de inseguridades.
La familia apoyo me dió.

A los dieciocho años
madre me convertí
de Monchito, mi bebito
que adoré en cuanto lo ví.

Tres años después
mi matrimonio falló.
Cambios drásticos ocurrieron
y de mi vida tomé cargo yo.

His timid glance of insecurity
entered my heart
like an ardent flame
of what we call love.

With his dark, curly hair
his jet-black eyes
his smile without malice
and his good manners—

"A good man," my father said,
"since he likes to work,
improve his future,
and support a home."

My mother said, "He's good looking
and has a good sense about him;
we will offer him conversation
and allow him to enter without fear."

Three days a week
he visited without fail
with my parents' supervision—
the time made him think.

He offered marriage
for the wedding he paid.
We joined as a couple
and that's how it began.

Six months after
I found myself pregnant
full of insecurities.
My family gave me support.

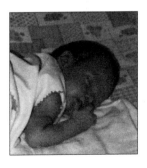

At eighteen years old
I became mother
of Monchito, my baby
whom I adored at first sight.

Three years later
my marriage failed.
Drastic changes occurred
and I took charge of my life.

AURA LUZ SANCHEZ

A LOVE STORY

NOTES : *Vieja*, old; *rebulu*, commotion; *la loca*, the crazy one; *Boricua*,
a term of endearment for Puerto Rico; *sofrito*, Puerto Rican
condiments; *iglesia*, church; *tierra morena*, red earth; *coquí*, a tree frog,
national symbol for Puerto Rico; *cantaleo*, a racket; *que hombre raro*,
what a rare man.

I. Elisa

It must have been that *vieja* from Calle Quintana
who sicced the evil eye on me
or simply callous fate who ignored my girlhood pleas.
Although it was me Eduardo loved,
it was Lara who'd have his child.

You should have heard the *rebulu* that night
in Barrio Balboa.
I carried on like Isabel, *la loca*,
whose mother locked her up
to save the neighbors' ears.
Despite the scandal, his family was relieved.
They were pure-bloods from Las Mesas,
majordomos of the 'Cane.
The "honorable" thing was done
while I, a nasty spot, was bleached out
almost completely.
And why not, weren't my features coarser then gravel,
my hair like the coils of an innerspring?
Africa and the Caribbean could not be washed
from my *Boricua* face—
that's how I came to leave.

No sooner had the smelly, crowded barrios that ring San Juan
drifted out of sight
than my world turned the color of battleships
in Mayaguez Bay.
The monotony of the churning waves
made me feel I was on
the slow spit of a roasting pig.

At last a tall, gray world rose up to greet me,
gray as my heart,
gray as the sooty clothes I'd come to wash on Saturdays
in *Nueva York*,
then hang on lines outside
to sun and flap too close to Jewish shirts, Italian pants—
clothes that did not know not to tangle with each other.

At sixteen I went to live with Cousin Rita,
do the mending, mind the children.
That's where I met Toñito, the merchant marine.
He cared for me—I knew it—
but I could only think of roosters crowing
and her womb growing to displace my memory.

Then one night he and I went out
to the *Teatro Hispano*,
returned late.
The streetlights had been working overtime,
outside the door my bags were packed,
orphans waiting on a doorstep.
My thwarted rage, like the lion's roar at Bronx Park Zoo,
got nowhere.
Hot shame flooded through my face,
my insides were as jumbled as the contents
of my cardboard valise.
So I went with him that night
—turned into thirty years
of pipes and kids and wondering
what if

II. Toñito

I might as well have been speaking in Tongues:
"New York is no place
to be raising chickens!"

To Elisa this was the city's failing,
to be waved away like an annoying fly.
To me, it was *the* domino
that would fell the other dominoes
of our married life.
What use was there in nagging,
she refused to store away

those phantoms
of her Puerto Rico past.
Like in a home crowded with relatives
I was forced to share our bed
with her estranging daydreams
of how life could have been with him.

She never fully crossed
the threshold of our marriage.
Elisa was an unfinished soul migrating,
searching for the ghosts
of younger days.

Yet through the yards of gauze
she wrapped about herself, we had
family together: can you smell
the five o'clock *sofrito*
for the evening meal,
hear the whirring of her Singer,
sewing lacy dresses for our little girls,
her mimicking of vendors
bellowing out their wares,
Ice, Watermelons, Newspapers—
collected by the rag man
in his horse-drawn cart,
galin-gilan, galin-gilan,
the clamoring bell of the *galin-gilan* man
who pedaled his cart down the cobbled street,
hauling his stone to sharpen scissors, knives, and tools.
The photo albums grew thick with
birthdays, communions, weddings.

After thirty years of marriage the Singer idled.
I—no longer able to be Samaritan
to her spirits, which sagged like beaten branches
in a hurricane—had grown an armadillo's hide;
that's when she left.

III. Eduardo

After mourning for Lara
I mourned for myself.
I reached maturity
without ever having blossomed.

Mine were seeds sown
by others; by *familia,*
iglesia, comunidad.
I graduated from a high school
where English-only was allowed;
teachers were imported
from the States.
I fell in love with Elisa,
a poor girl from the Barrio,
but at seventeen I had to marry Lara,
to save her honor.
I rose to Chief of Customs
for the port of Mayaguez.

After Lara died,
alone with whining cats,
my children grown and married,
I looked in vain for meaning
like a sailor with lost bearings
who looks for signs of shore—
land birds, floating branches.
I found none, only barren sea.

And then, condolences from
Elisa, after lost years of separation.
Delighted, my memories did a rhumba,
I sent her roses
across the ocean to that pitiful place
where flowers are doomed to bloom
one season only—*Nueva York.*

To be *un hombre* is to possess—
it is part of Spanish culture.
By simply staking flags
into dark-red *tierra morena*
Columbus made Spain
conquistadora of a whole new world.
Like Columbus, I demanded.
Elisa left Toñito and became my wife.

Then I met Toñito and
I understood the cost
of my penchant to possess;
I too had staked a flag
that had burrowed deep into another's sorrow.

There was no way to make amends
except to befriend
this extraordinary man.
That he could find such satisfaction
in simply visiting with us:
his only wish, to see that she was well.
Odd to see the three of us
sitting over coffee
enjoying the relief of evening air,
our conversation set to the music
of a hidden choir of *coquí.*

He and I would stay up almost to the time when roosters
start their *cantaleo,*
drinking Coronas, discussing La Prensa.
He had a mind as fertile as
the coral reefs off Boqueron.
I'd demand statehood,
he'd defend fanatic
Independentistas;
both of us critical
of *Pentecostales* with their *aleluyas*
and their tambourines.
We played dominoes; in chess
we took turns checking each other's kings.

Then, as in the card game of Casino,
we'd pick up and discard each other's tales.
He told me he was sixteen
when he stowed away
on a ship in old San Juan,
spent a spell with a brother in the Bronx.
But he'd inherited a wanderlust
from his grandfather-explorers
and soon was sailing as a merchant marine.
On leave, back home one day,
he met Elisa; they were married for thirty years
before my intrusion into their lives.

Que hombre raro was Toñito:
the dignity of a naked martyr nailed to a cross.
Rare because despite his woes
he was always aware
of branches floating, land birds flying over
fertile seas.

Li Min Mo

WE DROP OUR JAWS AND LAUGH TO HEAVEN

I.
We are led to believe that
this country is not ready for a woman
president because some people still think
the female race is always squabbling,
obsessed with shopping, their noses are
too close to their cooking pots, their ears
can't hear the divine sounds, their mouths
can't voice philosophical truths, their vision
is blurred by years of near-sighted habits.
Like mice, women seek comfort in hidden
crannies, the closets where their memories
are stored in bags, boxes, and old pocketbooks.

The '96 Olympic program announces that
". . . women want stories." All things have
stories—a sweater knitted by Grandmother
Flo, Jimmy's bowling trophies from
sixth grade, homemade Halloween costumes.
Women believe in saving things: recipes,
wishbones, good luck charms, blessings.
It's easy for a woman to spend hours in
the closet, indulging, taking secret
flights to her past and reliving
stories triggered by a tattered Snoopy won
at a country fair. Sometimes
after a secret retreat, women stagger out
drunk with nostalgia, their bodies shaking
with excitement, eyes deepened with knowing.

II.
Lately, Mother is worrying about me;
she shakes her head at my twenty-five
six-year-olds—more than a handful.
I teach my first graders to celebrate life: greet
each other in the mornings, share stories from
everyday living, clean up their own mess,
put things back on the shelves, wait for
their turn to speak; to take joy in a purple
tulip, a large flat speckled stone, a
ragged puppet, an old alphabet book.

It's rare that my mother and I
get together and do nothing.
One Sunday morning we sit
in the kitchen, our
busy hands weighed down by
chores now dancing. We
laugh; our roaring belly
sound clears our noses and ears.
Feeling our breath travel
to the sky, we drop our jaws.

We find ourselves sailing upon
a raft. The horizon is an
immense circle of billowing
clouds. Without restraint we
howl with the wind, wail with the storm,
squawk like albatrosses.
At last we set free
the wild laughter.

ELENA HARAP

LONELY SISTER BLUES

for Lynda Patton

Lynda, where are you?
I haven't had a good argument for weeks
I'm stuck in a balloon of self-importance
and no Lynda-baby to go popping it
with her irreverent intelligence

Lynda, I'm lonely.
But all sisters are lonely,
doing their work, loving their people,
dusting out a secret space
where poems happen

Hey Lynda, I'm listening.
I hear you in the kitchen on Deckard Street
and the smoke-sweet laughter
of my sister
filing her nails into elegant arches
and playing Earth, Wind, and Fire
is the breeze and sunshine
inside my head today

A SIMPLE THING THAT MAKES ME HAPPY

My lovable son Ramón wears clothes twice as big as he is. He listens to loud rap music—"Push it good, push it real good"—and is absolutely sure that the world owes him something. He is egocentric, believing that when he has a need I should forget all my responsibilities to attend to him. Ramón is the typical sixteen-year-old you see on TV, who loves cars and girls. He is skilled in baseball and basketball, but in school his grades are below average. And yet he says, "I am cool."

Somehow when we go to Jamaica Plain to his grandparents' house, he becomes human. My father is eighty years old, very small and frail, and he adores my son. Ramón, who is over six feet tall and weighs more than two hundred pounds, adores my father and pampers him. When we go to visit—which is very often—my father, who spends a lot of time sitting on the sofa, gets up to welcome his grandson. Ramón walks towards this old man and hugs him. Before separating from my father, he makes eye contact with him, holds his grandfather's head in his huge hands, and kisses him on the forehead. Ramón appears to be the father, holding his little child.

As I view this scene, my worries about my son melt.

MARY MILLNER McCULLOUGH

empty shell

i pick you up
beside a pile of empty houses
call you a clam
strike at your door
learn you are a mussel
ask forgiveness
and peer inside

i see landscapes from the moon
whales swimming
pearls birthing charcoal scars
monarchs flying with their shadows
snails carrying hearts in their eyes
moths imitating butterflies
frogs on lily pads croaking
purple bleeding into black

i see promises detained in jars
rocks break and smash
melt from kissing
green tones on stairs like milky glass
war outside darkened rooms
women waiting for lovers
sewing quilts with hair
children sitting still
playing with bombs
sleep shelters dug in the ground
leak soldiers needing repair

i see water wash over your back
return grains of sand
enter your mouth
like a cool flame in heat

AURA LUZ SANCHEZ

TO LIVE IN THE MARGINS

Notes: *Marquesina*, roofed entry in front of a house; *plena*, Puerto Rican traditional dance; *mira*, *muy bonita*, look, very pretty.

I was the captain of a schooner navigating between the latitudes and longitudes of two cultures. Balmy breezes lifted me high into meringue-shaped clouds. At other times, bewildering sea storms bashed me off course. The child of Puerto Rican immigrants, I came to fix my course on the one that would lead to Americanization, much to the consternation of my perplexed mother.

> *April was so far away,*
> *the once a year time when*
> *we would visit.*
> *If only visits were more casual,*
> *more frequent, not laden*
> *with so much expectation;*
> *tired bones, skin dry from the Mayaguez heat—*
> *it was important,*
> *would I come put her papers in order?*
>
> *Death, peering through the slats*
> *of the marquesina*
> *had inspired her to dust her fragile figurines.*

Her father's green-eyed ghost
was visiting more often now.
Would I come and talk with her,
the way she knew I did with my own daughter.
She'd see us every April
in the bedroom, carrying on
about nothing in particular;
something she had never done with us.

In exchange for a "better" life
she was seduced by the sweet promises
of earning a living in New York City
which like a beehive
ensured a dubious role for workers.
Here, she bred strangers
who spoke reluctant Spanish,
who understood
what she would never know
but who would never savor
her rice and beans
or sway to the rhythm
of her beloved plenas.
How could we,
daughters of an urban ghetto,
understand the ways of a Borinquen mother?
Our clocks ticked much too fast
for her mañanas,
and now she wondered
if I'd come talk with her
the way we never did.

Though the experts lend us their theories on the causes
and patterns of migration, it is the individual stories that fulfill our
need to understand and allow us to empathize with those who paid
the exorbitant cost of leaving their families and cultures behind. For
me the stories were about Celina, who sobbed in the cold of the
silent radiator and stared at a naked sky lacking leafy camouflage; of
Toñito, who had stowed away on a ship to come to America and
cried with other New Yorkers when Ebbetts Field was demolished;
of Titi, first generation, who could speak both languages but would

grow up not accepted by "the Americans" and alienated from the Puerto Ricans; and of Anelisa, who loved her grandmother but was frustrated by her own lack of Spanish and dismayed because she was unable to understand the treasures of her cultural past.

These were the stories I wanted to tell. I had grown up listening to my mother's stories about Juan Bobo, a seemingly dull-witted *jibaro* (a hick from the interior mountains of the island), and taking roles in the plays my sister Virginia made up, based on movies she had seen or books she had read. I looked forward to Virginia's evening performances as if they were opening nights on Broadway. Our bedroom was transformed into Spanish galleons, treasure islands, medieval walled cities.

When my sister was nine years old, she came home one day very excited and told me a secret: that instead of going out to play she had walked, like a pirate, carefully following her treasure map, the six or seven blocks that led to the neighborhood branch of the New York Public Library. "Imagine," she said, "they let you take books out for free!" I remember the day she took me along, the marvelous pink granite building, the many books my sister borrowed and then read to me each night. She made sure I signed up for my own library card. Years later when we moved to Brooklyn, I remember that one of the consolations of having to leave the Bronx and my beloved cousin Evelyn was that the public library was right around the corner. I didn't even have to cross streets to get there.

PART I

The moon bloated round, branded the sole of my newborn foot with the image of his face—at least that is how my mother explained the bright raspberry etching so conveniently concealed. Perhaps his mark was a reminder that I was not supposed to have been conceived. Five years earlier, my mother had almost died giving birth to my sister Virginia. A policeman had come to our apartment to tell my father his wife had died in childbirth. It was a mistake; but my parents were warned: no more babies or they might not be so lucky next time. I was born in 1941 in the Lincoln Hospital, a public hospital in the South Bronx. Perhaps in gratitude to the forces of nature for granting my mother another extension of life, my parents named me Aura Luz, Light of Dawn. What must have been going through my father's anxious heart the day they had been warned about, the day that I was born?

Black eyebrows arching over a gaze
whirlpooled in bewilderment;
his stony, seated figure
carved into the secondhand armchair
upstairs in Apartment Three.

Five years ago the policeman knocked,
an anti-Gabriel announcing
the birth of his first-born,
the death of his wife.
But the policeman was wrong—
a minor error in the public records
of Lincoln Hospital.

Death was a gambler playing a crap game.
The dice turned out in her favor.
The gambler moved on, leaving her
resurrected, in critical condition.
The doctors warned: no more babies.

Now he sits, a statue
in the barely lit living room
of Apartment Three,
awaiting the birth of his second child.
He'll be missed today by the guys
at Sunnyside train yard.

A cacophony still in his ears:
screams of labor, sirens taking her away.
Saliva dams up in his throat
as he recalls the near miss of five years ago,
adrenaline careers full speed
through the alleys of his body.

He imagines the delivery room:
her howls bouncing off
the hospital's peeling green walls;
a rat peering out from the corner
observing a child who was not supposed
to be born.

My parents emigrated from Puerto Rico in their teens and met in New York. My mother, Elisa, came to take care of her cousin's children and to heal a broken heart. My father, restless to see the world, stowed away twice on a ship before he arrived in the city. After they were married, they lived in the Barrio, an Upper East Side ghetto in Manhattan. By the time I was born, they were living in the South Bronx. I remember my mother taking us food shopping back in the Barrio, at La Marketa—a series of buildings with indoor stalls running about half a mile of city streets, tucked under the tracks of the New York Central, where suburban commuters could gape fleetingly, safely, at the slums. Clothes, toys, fish, vegetables, radios, canaries, bedspreads, and other items were sold. The vendors, all gringos, were rough and dirty, their stalls smelly. "Mira, mira, muy bonita," they'd say in pidgin Spanish to get your attention. Despite the disheveled appearance of the stalls, it was always an adventure to go shopping in La Marketa.

Growing up in the Forties and Fifties, I remember a trail of relatives coming and staying with us before finding their own apartments. My parents would greet relatives, friends, even casual visitors, with the saying, "Mi casa es tuya,"—my house is yours—the customary greeting Puerto Ricans took pride in saying and carrying out; and one that my individualistic American personality resented terribly when it meant having to share the Ellis Island of my maple bed with the tired cousins who came through our apartment door. My sister and I condescendingly referred to these cousins as "Marine Tigers," Nuyoriquen for Puerto Rican newcomers. (The original Marine Tiger was a ship that brought many Puerto Ricans to New York in the early 1940s). Somehow the cousins managed to arrive with their parents at La Guardia airport in the middle of the night, the boys dressed in mannish hats and ties, the girls in frilly dresses and patent leather shoes. They always ended up having to sleep with me. Even so, middle-of-the-night trips to the airport, with its WPA murals and constant flow of relatives, were always thrilling. As I got older I came to appreciate the hardships these relatives experienced as new immigrants in the many-chaptered story of the American migration.

One of these relatives was my brother, originally my cousin. My mother's brother Mon and his wife Milagros came from Puerto Rico in 1947 with their six-month-old son, Ramón. Milagros was sixteen. She was not very happy when she came to live with us, and within three months had deserted her husband and son. We never heard from her again. Mon was a *macho*, a womanizer, and was neither willing to provide for a nine-month-old nor capable of doing so. My mother began taking care of Ramón for her brother. Before long she had grown extremely attached to Junior, as he came to be called. We began to think of him as our brother and he readily called my parents *Mami* and *Papi*.

Periodically Mon would show up, but no one ever told my brother Ramón about his biological parents, so protective was my mother of him; no one, that is, except my cousin Papo, who was about Junior's age. When they were both about seven years old, Papo overheard from the family that Junior "did not belong" to my parents. "Elisa's not your real mother, nyah, nyah, nyah, nyah," he thoughtlessly blurted out once or twice when he was angry at Junior for having beaten him in a game of cards. Virginia and I became concerned that Junior would continue to hear about his origins in less than favorable ways, and we prevailed upon my mother to tell him the truth. She finally acquiesced. I remember the day when we called my brother into the living room, interrupting his race down the stairs to go out and play stick ball, and told him the story of his birth. My mother, my sister, and I were crying and trying to assure him that we loved him and that he would always be our brother. After we were through with the emotional revelation, Junior responded simply by saying, "Now can I go out and play stick ball?"

We lived on the first floor of an old building in a neighborhood in transition. The once-thriving synagogues were losing their congregations. Many were being boarded up or recycled as fundamentalist, Pentecostal churches for the Latino newcomers; Hebrew characters permanently carved on stone over-arched the plywood crosses of the burgeoning *Iglesias de Dios*. My father worked for the Pennsylvania Railroad and, when working the day shift, arrived home every day about 5:30 PM. My sister and I ran to meet him at the Jackson Avenue subway stop, anxious to be the first one to catch a glimpse of his wool cap adorned with AFL-CIO union buttons. He was a staunch social-democrat who believed in men like FDR, Vito Marcantonio, and Jackie Robinson. He was hardly down the long flight of stairs when we started questioning him. "Did anything interesting happen on the trains today? Did you find anything for us, *Papi*?" He was responsible for many odd jobs at the Railroad, including cleaning out the trains after they pulled into their final destination at Sunnyside Yard in Queens. Objects he happened to find while cleaning the trains were turned in to the Lost and Found. After a certain claims period had elapsed, he could keep the found items. Once he found a black doll with a basket of bananas glued to her dark, curly hair. She was black and beautiful, and I named her Désirée, after a movie I had seen about Napoleon.

My childhood memories are of hours spent playing street games—ring-o-levio, hopscotch, jump rope games, ball games, Time, King of the Mountain—of roller skating and picnicking at St. Mary's park in the Bronx, of Saturday nights with relatives gathered at our house, singing, dancing, playing *loteria* (bingo), and playing guitars. Christmas Eve and New Year's Eve were always holidays for large family get-togethers. As teenagers, we were allowed to go to New Year's parties, but only if we made sure we were home by midnight. I remember running home to be with my family, only to run back to the party after welcoming the New Year.

Celebrating the arrival of the New Year was a solemn, almost religious occasion, a time for remembering family members who had died. It was said that sometimes, if the dead were forgotten, they would come back to haunt us by inhabiting the bodies of the living. My mother's sisters were especially adept at going into trances where spirits, *espiritos*, would inhabit their bodies and speak through them. For us children it was scary, but also fascinating. These trance attacks, *ataques* as they were called, often occurred on New Year's Eve, causing pandemonium.

I remember one New Year's when my cousin Evelyn had received permission to stay over at my house. There was a big party going on. Adults and children were dancing, playing guitars, playing games—a truly festive occasion—when out of some primordial nowhere, one by one, three of my mother's sisters began moaning, entering into a trance. The music stopped. Everyone hovered around them. One of my aunts' husbands slapped his wife and yelled at her to leave behind these *boberias*, idiocies. Eventually they all snapped out of their *ataques*, but by then my cousin was no longer allowed to stay the night.

Paquita's writhing face
was spewing gibberish voices,
it was New Year's Eve,
la vispera del año nuevo.

The family's dead
were party-crashing:
un demonio trapped on a cobweb
somewhere in Paquita's mind.

This espirito meant no harm,
its ay-ay-ay a plea
not to be forgotten.
It would soon be moving on,
the fiesta would resume;

a sober New Year would reflect
on Cuba Libres, midnight hugs,
unresting rhythmic feet—and
el ataque de Paquita.

We moved from the Bronx to Brooklyn while I was in my teens. My memories of Brooklyn are of dances and romance, a time when everything that ever happened to you or around you was supposed to be a source of laughter, a joke; a time when irreverence peaked and you made faces behind the teacher's back; when all seemed ridiculous, especially the tastes and conversations of adults; when being loud and conspicuous was to be admired by your peers. It was a time of minimal involvement with studies and of inextricable ties with friends whom I could not bear to be away from for more than a day. I rarely missed school because that was where I'd see them. And I never missed a day of "hanging out"; to do so was like having your leg fall asleep: a part of you was not quite there. My friends were Puerto Rican, Italian, Irish, and Norwegian, but there were no Jews or blacks where we lived. It was diverse ethnically and homogeneous economically; we were all working-class poor.

I remember the time when my friends and I were returning from Coney Island Beach after having a great time dipping our feet in the water and dancing under the boardwalk. We were on our way home on the BMT subway, having a hard time settling down, when we broke into singing "Bye, Bye, Love" by the Everly Brothers. Everyone on the train joined in, clapping and singing—it was like a stage set for a Broadway musical. Only three or four stations out, New York's finest came in and brought the curtain down, pulling my cousin Evelyn, the star of the cast, and Wilma, my friend, out of the train. We were so scared we got giddy. We waited for what seemed like forever, at the Fifty-fourth Street stop, for them to show up. Finally they came, laughing and rolling their eyes. We couldn't wait to talk about it. They had been read the riot act and put on the next train. To us, this was one of the highs of the summer.

As the metamorphosis from adolescents to young adults took place, our indivisibility began to fracture, at first by the duality of our dreams. Mine were of getaways from the griminess of gray concrete lives, theirs of wedding aisles leading to tiled kitchens and umbrella strollers. Few of my friends graduated from high school. Many of the girls became pregnant before they stopped being teenagers.

I was on a different track even then. Although I always knew I would go on to college, I down-played my aspirations around the neighborhood. I had already gotten a reputation for being a straight-A student, which had lots of negative connotations—if you were brainy, it was thought you were not spontaneous, not brave, wouldn't know how to be zany and crazy, and probably didn't know how to have fun. Eventually the tracks could no longer cross.With a smothering sense of loss, I realized that I had outgrown my friends. I knew I'd have to break with them or give up my dreams of a world beyond the neighborhood.

I graduated from Bay Ridge High School with a small scholarship to Brooklyn College. It was the only college I applied to that I knew I could attend for free. In those days Brooklyn College, later to become part of the City University of New York, admitted only New York residents graduating from high school with a high grade point average. Despite my meeting the qualifications, the transition from high school and neighborhood to college was like a book with the middle chapters torn out. I was an immigrant in the land of higher education. I had to struggle with a new language and culture. I was woefully unprepared to negotiate in the arena of liberal arts. My vocabulary had never wandered outside of my neighborhood. I admired those with facility in this culture: the Irish boy from Flatbush in freshman English who had read *Ulysses*, could discuss its symbolism in his Brooklynese, and always wore a brown

Eisenhower jacket; the Jewish boy who sent me love letters in perfect French and fantasized that he was Orpheus and I, Euridice. By my senior year I was engaged to be married to the Irish boy from Flatbush, who had by then stopped wearing his Eisenhower jacket and was preparing to go to law school.

PART II

Jim and I were married after graduation from college. We barely looked back as we embraced a new existence in Cambridge, Massachusetts. Behind us were our working-class, city college, and blue-collar neighborhoods; ahead, the ivy walls of Harvard. My husband had been accepted at Harvard Law School—a boarding pass to another life. At last I could escape the film of poverty and grime that tenaciously clung to us in Brooklyn, the monotonous diet of *arroz con abichuelas* (rice and beans), the nauseating smell of *bacalau* (fried cod), the superstitious beliefs of my family, the snares of a neighborhood which held my friends captive in the resin of teen motherhood and dead-end jobs. Before long we were caught up in the values of the Cambridge elite. Our must-have list included travel to Europe, English bone china, corporate partnership on Wall Street. It was a heady time, and I was still too young to understand that, in turning my back on the essence of who I was, I might never again experience its comfort. Years later I would find myself in therapy, celebrating my academic successes and the quality of life I had achieved, but also in pain over the loss of a culture and community I had cheated on, walked out on, only to find them not home when I was ready to crawl back in.

After Jim's law school graduation, we went to Lima. He was on a fellowship to study land use planning; I got a job with an anthropological institute interested in cross-cultural studies. We became friendly with Peruvian revolutionaries and American Peace Corps volunteers. By this time our marriage had taken an irretrievable turn into a cul-de-sac. We both realized we had different cultural expectations, clashing personalities, polar political perspectives, and had married too young. Climbing the breathtaking heights of Macchu Picchu, bartering for hand-woven rugs in Ayacucho, sipping tropical drinks in the stultifying heat of the Amazon, we began drifting further and further apart. Before our drift had reached oceanic proportions we would conceive Dylan, our son.

Against the backdrop of the Poor People's March on Washington, race riots, and the mobilization of a generation at war with their parents' values, I became a mother. After Peru, Jim had taken a job at the newly created Department of Housing and Urban Development. The year was 1968, the hallmark year of the counter-culture rebellion throughout America and the Western world, a year adorned with love beads and ethnic clothes, scented with the ubiquitous waft of marijuana. While others my age were engaged in confrontation over a "dirty little war," I took refuge inside my pregnant shell, my thoughts confined to the child I was carrying, obsessed with abdominal breathing and the Lamaze method of childbirth. I ignored the sounds of angry throngs outside my window during the race riots that summer, so engrossed was I in Dr. Spock's chapter on nursing.

Occasionally, reality would insinuate itself into my consciousness and force me to think about my troubled marriage, which was unraveling like missed stitches of a knitted sweater. Mostly I succeeded in being oblivious, floating trance-like through nine months in Washington, D.C., daydreaming about whether my baby would have blue eyes or brown, sleepwalking to the local Kresge's to buy baby T-shirts. Dylan was born at Georgetown University Hospital. He was five months old when I left Jim and Washington and moved back to Boston.

There is a John Denver song which goes, "He was born in the summer of his twenty-seventh year." The line has always intrigued me because I like to think that I too was spiritually born in my twenty-seventh year. For the six years of my marriage I had allowed another person to become more important, more equal, than I. His career, his interests, his values, were what mattered in our young graduate lives. I worked so he could go to school; we both rationalized that he was struggling through law school so that eventually we could both enjoy the "good American life." Jim argued well, and we made the mistake of thinking that logic somehow equated truth.

In my South End apartment with my son, that year, the enigma of my existence haunted me. A failed marriage, a baby, and no job: what had I become? It was time to put an end to these debilitating feelings. My soul, shrouded in ambiguities, shed its gauzy wrappings, giving birth to the person I wanted to be. It would be many years before this person learned to stand on her own two feet, but it was enough that at least she was toddling.

I thought about the time when, at eleven, I was finally able to realize my dreams and go see where my mother was from; I visited my grandmother in Puerto Rico, meeting her and many other relatives for the first time. My cousins laughed at me because the soles of my feet were too soft, needing the protection of shoes, and because I wore a big, conspicuous straw hat to church instead of the more subtle mantilla. I remember feeling like a misfit, wanting to cry and return home. I thought back to the nuns of St. Anselm's, who made my sister and me feel as welcome as Jehovah's Witnesses, though we kicked higher than most colleens, doing the obligatory Irish jig, and our hearts were all shamrock on St. Patrick's Day. I had been too young then to understand the dilemma of people caught between the magnetic poles of two cultures. The trick was to see them as not in conflict with each other, but rather as complementary alchemy. First generation was neither mainstream American nor New World Puerto Rican. Whatever the amalgam, it was every bit as legitimate as its parent cultures. I would no longer allow myself to apologize for being unauthentically American or Puerto Rican; for not being the "real thing." Rather I would celebrate the American multicultural phenomenon of being "first generation."

That twenty-seventh year I found myself repeatedly thinking about my early life. I missed my childhood, and I missed the laughter and word play of my mother and my aunts. My mom would finish off the ad tune for Motorola TV with, "Llevala al hospital," take her to the hospital, purposely misconstruing TV as TB. If I complained about a headache, dolor de cabeza, she'd tell me, "Metate debajo de la mesa," get under the table, only because la mesa rhymed with cabeza. I longed to relive those days in the Bronx when my parents would have parties with everyone invited, children and all, and to hear my father play the guitar and sing "Tu, solo tu," a popular Mexican song, followed by a Mexican yell. I longed for the summer days when we would all pile into the back of Uncle Cristobal's pick-up truck, from which he used to sell fruit, and go to the East River to play games the men would make up, such as trying to ring an old tire around the branch of a tree. Every time my father threw the tire he would yell, "Co-ordination!" Sometimes at night we'd go to a forgotten little graveyard and party. I missed going to Orchard Beach and Pelham Bay, where my mother's idea of a picnic was a big potful of rice and beans. At the Spanish movies she took us to, she thought nothing of bringing soup into the dark movie house, making sure we always had a nourishing lunch. And I missed the shy little girl I had been, learning English, responding to "What's your name, little girl?" by answering, "Titi Sanchez," and to "Where do you live, little girl?"

and every other question in English with the same words, "Titi Sanchez."

I learned to love my Puerto Rican roots even as I came to understand that I was very much east-coast American with an Irish Catholic elementary schooling and a baccalaureate from a predominantly Jewish city college. I came to appreciate my Taino cheekbones, my Spanish name, the Caribbean emotions that flowed through my veins. I knew I had to write about the community I had abandoned, recapture a lifestyle that would soon become a quick blip on the historic screen.

What had triggered these epiphanies? Epiphanies are the exclamation points of life, amidst the declarations and question marks that punctuate the mysteries of the universe. Perhaps my mystical rebirth was caused by my becoming a mother for the first time, reflecting on how different the life of my child, product of a first generation Puerto Rican and a third generation Irish-American, would be from mine and from his grandparents'. Perhaps it was the halcyon days of the Sixties, when world values and world order, like the "flatness" of the earth centuries earlier, were being subjected to scrutiny by those who had never been allowed to look through the telescope—native Americans, women, welfare mothers, minorities, and others, all of whom were causing cataclysmic paradigm shifts throughout the Western world. I too would commit heresy and declare myself an equal.

Jim and I eventually divorced. I remarried, had two other children, and went to law school. It wasn't until after I began working as an attorney that I began to write, mostly narrative poems about the immigrant experience. I have always understood that my poems revealed more about myself than about the relatives and friends who were my subjects. What I have learned recently is that writing transformed me, giving me a better understanding of culture and its conflicts. While living in the margins was often confusing, it gave me a wide-angle perspective because I could look out with two different sets of lenses.

Her fanciful gaze wafts away
to a place where her mother was born,
a place she has never seen.
She imagines a grove of mangoes,
flamboyan in the hair
of coquí colored trees.
Caribbean sea nymphs
beckon her to this mystical place
in the sun.

Reality intrudes with the hissing of steam
and the odor of fried bacalau.
Outside, the frost is deprived
of the day's elongated shadows;
its playmate the sun lazily lies
in the lap of some gray-bloated cloud.

People crunched up
in their coats
walk grimly along city streets.

She seeks solace once more
in the place where her mother was from.
There, she does not exist in the margins
of two peoples, two colors, two tongues.
No apologies there
for her coffee complexion,
her unamerican nose;
no English or Spanglish to fear,
no Marine Tigers to share
her small bed with,
no freckle-faced girls
to cause tears.
The warming womb
of imagination
transports her once more
to her mystical place in the sun.

Testimonies

Mary Millner McCullough

news from eden

a howling processional
parades on fourth of july in america
brownie scouts follow drum majorettes
behind baseball diamonds on floats
dignified pipers dressed in stars and stripes
of twenty-four american flags from lost and found

daughters of the american revolution
humming braveheart tunes
the best sort of patriotism

democracy laid down strong
ideas stitched into a quilt gone wrong

are we blessed or damned
living here
on this island in the sun
impotent in the shadows
cast by weight shifting on shimmering sand

oak bluffs and roxbury mindlocked as black towns
spill over from circuit street to south beach
from dudley station to the merry-go-round

high profile well-behaved crowds
at inkwell beaches
in boston taxis
riding the surf
and subways

hip hop singers
hairdressing executives
clothing store clerks wearing football jerseys
select black men
released from the academy
dancing to a latin beat on mass avenue

watch the blending
say amen to the mix
there's a white guy
and a blonde or two

twenty thousand gather
on south beach
three days straight through the summer night
flashy revelers, rap groups, video clowns,
police are called
inner city gangs crossing vineyard sound
they heard there's a party
in edgartown

tolerance stretched thin
citizens respond
no get it all straight
no gangs here
quell racial overtones
nice people
those african americans
too bad when they come in a crowd
we have to be ready
to keep public safety   control

it's really a community problem
make a resolution
get the real estate people
no more than ten on the beach
five on the ferry
one of each on the street
none in our school

not a problem if they choose
that cultural thing not on the police list of duties
their history and all that
it's just the numbers
that causes the alarm
disrupts our quiet
comes creeping
disturbing our community resolve

the nun warns immigrants
freedom doesn't come easy
and the preacher tells his god
he had a dream
then asks
who is the devil responsible
for the typos appearing in my reams

contorted squares in blue bottle frames
trap voices whispering
better take lessons, take lessons, take lessons
get ready for the hurricane

the world's dressed waiting for an insanity cure
while naked men found walking north
are arrested for decent exposure

revived drunk driver's feet run
on sleeping man in road

floating empty truck
picks up body

911 called
deliver to docks
next of kin notice

oh, joyous celebration
black-eyed susans
have come to eden

Aura Luz Sanchez

NOT MACHO ENOUGH

Note: *Status offense,* wrongdoing defined simply by
identity rather than by any specific action.

my misdemeanor: I am not macho enough

the list of particulars:
> I don't speak with the unhesitating authority
> > of a white man;
> do not pontificate or have all the answers;
> do not interrupt speakers
> or adhere to a Ptolemaic theory of myself;
> do not ignore my sixth sense;
> do think emotional vulnerability
> > is a sign of strength

that I think in ellipses instead of lines
that my weavings have texture
my colors have shade
that I know how to listen
prefer question marks to exclamation points
am not in love with the pronoun "I"

these are my status offenses

BLANCA'S ARRIVAL IN THE WORLD

My mother, María Veléz de Bonilla, is a very strong woman. She walks with a straight posture that portrays control and authority, even though humility and kindness radiate from her. My father, Rafael Bonilla, small, soft-spoken, and mysterious, has the ability to control the household. I was born on September 7, 1961, making the ninth child. My mother had a very hard time bringing me into the world. But—as she stated—"The harder the labor is, the better off you are," meaning that I would be priceless. She did all the suffering in the beginning, therefore she would enjoy the best of me. She had contractions for a couple of days. Of course she waited until she finished with the housework. Finally I was pounding, "Get me out! It's too dark in here. I am ready." She could not bear it any more and asked my father to take her to the hospital in Lares, which was miles from our house.

When she arrived, the doctor did the regular checkup and told her that she was not ready to have the baby. She told him that she knew her body and that she was going to deliver that night. As he was walking out of the room, he said, "I am the doctor and I know better. If you want to stay, that is your problem. You are not having that baby yet." My mother was furious. She was having contractions and holding on to herself. In the meantime I was kicking and screaming, "Get me out of here!" She lost consciousness and woke up the following morning in a big room filled with hospital beds. A nurse approached her and congratulated her. "You had a baby girl last night. You need to give her a name as soon as possible." My mother realized that she did not have a name for me. The nurse brought an almanac and showed her the names for the month of September. Most of the names were already in the family. That's how I ended up with the name Blanca.

AURA LUZ SANCHEZ

THE SCHOOLYARD
All Souls' Day, November 2, 1950

Notes: Compadres, comadres, godfathers, godmothers—a close
relationship among these adults is implied; *compañeros*,
companions; *visabuelos*, great-grandparents, ancestors; *el* Yunque, a
mountain rain forest in Puerto Rico, largest tropical rain forest in
the Caribbean; *el Jíbaro*, rural people representing the folk culture of
Puerto Rico and symbolizing national pride; *grito*, scream.

With one-way airline tickets
in their pockets, they said A *Dios*
to Puerto Rico,
two patriots inexorably driven.
Torresola and Collazo would meet again
on the Willis Avenue Bridge in the Bronx,
map out secret plans
to expose the oppression
of their kept Antillean island.

On Halloween Day, 1950,
they made their way to the Blair House,
temporary quarters for President Truman.
Guns jammed; bullets misfired!
Torresola and a guard were killed,
Collazo sentenced to life, refusing to plea
for the mercy which would set him free.

November 2, 1950,
a parochial schoolyard in the Bronx:
the reported attempt on the President's life
fizzled,
inciting Kathleen's xenophobic cries.
My brown hand, trapped
inside her white one
like a moth in its cocoon,
squirmed to be set free.
Two by two we marched
into St. Anselm's schoolyard.
Scarlet rivulets of blood
raced up my cheeks.

Her words lingered long after,
like ugly blue despised tattoos.

"Death to all Porto Ricans—except
you, my dear. "
My rage bounced
off the insides of my head
as we continued our march, two by two,
into St. Anselm's Church
for All Souls' Day mass.
My body, steeped in sickness,
longed to dissipate
into the cool November air,
haunted by visions of dangling
compadres and *comadres* dying,
of grandmothers and grandfathers
hammered onto crosses,
of strung-up nieces and nephews
all because of *compañeros* like Torresola and Collazo,
who dared to dream
of independence
from the unrelenting grip
of my schoolyard friend.

What hurt words would spurt out
if I encountered her today;
what words would gush forth
with the force of water from a hydrant
uncorked by city kids
on a steamy summer day?
What words,
cooling decades of my pent-up rage?

"I am more than just
your schoolyard friend;
I am, will always be,
the mountainous cheekbones
of my *visabuelos*,
whose rugged peaks display the flags
of many peoples;
el Yunque with its wreath of stormy clouds;
el Jíbaro, whose *grito*,
like the croaking sounds of the *coquí*,
electrifies the countryside
. . . more than just your schoolyard friend."

MARY MILLNER McCULLOUGH

ALBERT

comes to school
no books
no pencils
no paper
no mortar for his bricks

between bells
his lithe frame weaves and struts
down the long corridor
his brown face frozen smooth—
a mind's imagined newborn fool

a major prop
a plastic tooth comb
like a solitary purple tree
crowns him prince

Albert pirouettes to the beat in his head
kisses girls
greets friends
gets the latest news since homeroom

teachers' nets screaming
passions and righteous words
meant to inspire
to motivate
float away on stale air
can't capture the boy
practicing to be a lover
in their hallways of learning

Albert leaves us missing him
blaming our books
a glut of reruns
starring dead white men
and black men's skeletons
stuck in the glory dance

of yesterday's revolution
retreat to shelves
waiting for Albert
to put meat on their bones

Albert
elusive   like dreams we surrender
before the sun cracks open the day
dances on
out the door
out of school
gone to love his girlfriend
and her mama

BLANCA BONILLA

REACHING DREAMS

Note: In the summer of 1997 I had the opportunity to manage a softball team for girls from the greater Boston area. Most of the girls had never played before. It was a challenge for all of us. The following poem was composed with Lissette Suárez, a team member.

The light in our eyes makes us believe we want to succeed—
we'll run that extra mile for anyone on our team.

We have our ups and downs with each other sometimes,
but we realize that without one another our team wouldn't be whole.

We all are individuals, that's what makes us unique,
with different attitudes that give our team a high peak.

Let us not forget the people behind the scenes—
our manager, our coach, and all of those great people
who cheer for our team,
to help us keep on going and reach our dreams.

Out there on the field
we play to win, we play with enthusiasm,
to beat the other team.

The pitcher on the mound
complains about the dust.
"My clothes are getting dirty
and my nails are breaking off."

As we look back,
we see our growth.
What a long way we have come
because the girls just wanted to play ball!

We feel we are breaking the barriers
against girls playing ball.
We are doing it for our future,
we are doing it for our souls.

LI MIN MO

NIGHT RIVER

Excerpt from a memoir in progress

If I don't descend into the purgatory, then who will go down for me?

Pregnant with my first child, I left my New York art world. A friend moved me from midtown Manhattan to Cambridge, Massachusetts. He tied my huge oil paintings on top of his VW van; somewhere along the way, all my paintings of naked ladies flew away. I unloaded my marble sculptures, two Kuen Yins reclining on their sides. I put the carvings in front of my apartment, tucked away behind a big building off Columbia Street. The next morning I discovered my goddesses of mercy stolen.

Holding my first born, I felt like a lost woman. Re-reading Dr. Spock five times didn't help with the postpartum blues. I broke up with my boyfriend, an intensely self-absorbed mathematician who rarely paid attention to me. When my son was barely one, I moved into a warehouse, formerly a piano factory and now a home to artists and light industry. A young man I met in a natural food store in Cambridge let me stay with him; that one night led to twenty-five years. I found something in him that mirrored myself: his deeply suppressed anger. Cloaked under a tragic aura was a sad, abandoned child.

The dark loft had no running water or bathroom facility. Down the dimly lit hall was a filthy public toilet and a slow-dripping fountain. Each day I lapsed into blackouts or suffered severe bouts of narcolepsy. I became completely disconnected with the world. Shadows of death stalked my movements and a powerful tremor shook my roots.

Those dark days in the warehouse brought back memories of my mother. When we first settled in New York in the early Sixties, she would break down after receiving onionskin-thin letters from her relatives. Each page fell from her hands as she wiped her tears. The river turned red, choked by the slaughtered bodies of the innocent. The yellow sheets were spirits, aborted flights, ghosts without names. She stood in front of her desk, which was cluttered with notebooks, paper and magazines, with a blank stare, her mouth twisted in pain. When I questioned curiously, *who, what, where,* I got the howl of a battle cry. *"Ai-ya, ni-tze-do-sen-mo," what do you know?* I must have sounded like a hostile intruder charging into her dungeon, where the walls were crumbling while the ground quaked. Around this time famine was spreading in the countryside of mainland China, followed by the insane Cultural Revolution. The letters that got smuggled out were like dying breaths, each tiny word a battle scar. Their silent testimony made her shout, rant, and curse. Night became a tormentor, a blood-thirsty demon.

The light was so dim in the kitchen that I could see only her back, bending into the tub, scrubbing, beating the washboard. The night became the Yellow River and its seasonal flooding, marking the history of the Chinese civilization. Everything was submerged under a watery vision. I heard my mother whisper the names of those who died a wrongful death, and she tried to show a little mercy to them by calling their names so their lost souls might find the way back to the ancestral burial ground. Water ghosts are known to be the most vengeful and difficult to appease. My mother's groans and muttering choked me. Frozen in listening, I huddled in the bed, pulling the quilt over me; I wished that I could become as tiny as a cockroach and sneak behind the walls.

The minute I dozed off, I sank into nightmares. All I could hope for was a special gesture or a magical word I once had known, but had now forgotten, that would lift me out of the chasm of abandonment. Tossing out of bad dreams, I woke to her sobbing—and in her pauses, a thick and ghastly silence. She addressed each relative by title, "Your great-grandmother hanged herself when they took the rest of her family to the village commons to get tortured, your great aunts . . . those women hanged themselves, some jumped into the family well. The peasants fed feces to your uncles who were the big landowners, pelted stones at your cousins, tortured each one to death . . . and your father—executed, executed, executed."

I still have trouble sleeping when I recall those hours; the tortured sounds she made became shrapnel embedded under my skin. How could I ignore her surging sorrow? She had no intention of passing down her memory to me or transferring the wounded relatives from her back to mine. Maybe I could have eased her burden, but she didn't teach me how to talk to the dead or to appease their anguish. Night after night, her fragmented recounting punished my fourteen-year-old body, a body that yearned for the romantic side of things, for something new. All I got then was a mother at the edge of the river, spilling her guts out.

How could one woman carry within her all the cries of her people, the unrelenting images of war, the blood of the wounded on her tongue? Some nights I questioned why she had to dislodge all these terrible things. Now, tracing over those nights, I have come to conclude that she was a victim of depression. She buried herself in work and pinned all her hope on her children. She cloistered herself, rarely inviting a friend over or talking to someone on the telephone. Immigrating to America, leaving behind her relatives, friends, and the writers' community—both in Taiwan and in mainland China— had made her a lost alien.

Hours later my mother would stumble into her bedroom, leaving me with a restless mind and body. A thousand strands of tangled sentiments, how could I begin to unravel them without making more knots? Those ghosts whom my mother didn't appease, I had to reckon with. They reminded me of the black-and-white footage I saw on TV, of the Japanese invasion of China during World War II—Chinese people fleeing the bombing raids in a mass exodus to the countryside, *tao-nan*. The mob surged forward, flesh pressing upon flesh until I could not distinguish a single face or expression, nothing but a bleak world thick with blood, tears, mud, and the legacy of war.

Those nights in the Lower East Side, listening to the voice of Purgatory, I thought about death by drowning, letting fish consume me. But the instinct to survive made me reach out for a life raft, or anything that would keep me from sinking. We didn't have a radio or a record player, and it was too late to turn on the black-and-white TV. The only thing we had plenty of were Chinese books; they lined a whole wall in my mother's bedroom. Days didn't fare better than nights, since I couldn't speak English or converse with other Chinese girls, who spoke Cantonese or Toisanese. School-days were alienating, except at music and art classes, where I could express myself. The minute I got home I would devour my mother's collection. I loved the translations of Turgenev's novels, especially *On the Eve*, but I was terrified by Dostoevsky's *Crime and Punishment*. I had a difficult time getting into my mother's favorite, Dreiser's *Sister Carrie*. There were novels, short stories, and plays by Chinese contemporary masters—Lao She, Lu Xuen, Xao Yu, Ba Qing. These great storytellers sustained my life, their words potent elixirs concocted by saints and immortals.

One night, to help me keep afloat on the turbulent river, I picked Roman Rolland's *Beethoven*, translated into Chinese. I kept it under my pillow for weeks. I hadn't heard of Beethoven's music, but I was deeply moved by his life—filled with pain and anguish—and by the way he channeled his passion into musical exultation. I thought, if this man kept composing, plucking his heart strings under harsh conditions, then I should go on dreaming, drawing, and singing, and one day I would escape.

When I was in tenth grade, my friend George played me a record of Beethoven's music. I broke down crying. I knew the great composer intimately; his soul had kept me from drowning and given me hope. His music opened the gate to the miraculous. Beethoven had held my head, supported my pillow with his strong hands that could unlock eighty-eight keys.

My mother's sorrow, an everywoman's lament, surges with the Yellow River and history of China, a counterpoint to Beethoven, whose spirit flows through the Danube. Night Rivers are tributaries that merge in the center of the geography of our souls.

* * *

I became pregnant again, and this time the man I lived with wanted me to get rid of it. He was not ready to be responsible and neither was I. To get a legal abortion I filled out tons of paper work, took tests, endured interrogations and interviews at the hospital. I blanked out at all the sessions; even during an interview with the psychiatrist I nodded off. After I got back from the hospital, my days became bleaker and darker. Each morning, rolling across the bed felt like navigating the Yangtze Gorge. I wanted to vomit all the time, but I couldn't find my mouth. Finally, I pushed myself up and sat at the edge of the bed with dread. I couldn't read or listen to music. I lay in the bottom of the river, bloated, unable to sound out a wail or howl; a drowned ghost stalked my movements. There was no one I could confide in. When I told people that I had been diagnosed as a narcoleptic, they looked at me as if I had mentioned leprosy. Even now, when I walk into a small room that gets no sunlight, I get a shudder in my heart.

In contrast to my sad condition, my one-year old son was exceptionally focused, quiet, and self-driven. Every day he constructed castles, huge structures, stacking cans on top of pots, pans, and wood blocks. Sometimes I would become transfixed by his creations, the joy of living in his sweet face. I thought there was life left in me still.

When the city took over the warehouse, we moved to a small apartment in Cambridge. Two years later, we moved into a rambling old farmhouse. All the rooms were large and in the day they were filled with sunlight.

I gave birth to a second child. My daughter was a beautiful, strong, and chubby baby. We were at a picnic at Fresh Pond one day and a neighbor's child was pushing the stroller. I knew something was wrong when I noticed my one-year old's face, pale and inattentive. That night she had a high fever and refused to eat. Finally she even vomited water. We rushed her to the hospital, and doctors told us we got there just in time to save her life. She had spinal meningitis. When I called my mother in New York, she blamed my daughter's illness on my hippie, unsanitary lifestyle. I was determined to make my child get well. I blended organic whole grains and vegetables into baby food and brought it to the hospital, feeding her for a whole month. Suddenly I felt as if I had a mission in life, and I found strength I had not had before. Every day I went around to talk about spinal meningitis with nurses and doctors, strangers in the lobby, even people I met while waiting for the bus. I inquired about the illness until I became convinced that my personality and my lifestyle were not the cause.

I started growing vegetables in my back yard, teaching art in after-school programs, and catering. I invented vegetarian recipes. The essence of seeds, flowers, legumes, whole grains, spices, and herbs guided my life. My days were stripped down into neat, rational order. To me, reading a cookbook was like engaging in meditation or the process of alchemy. I celebrated each holiday by creating a new sauce. Each year I put my craving for artistic outlet into my kids' birthdays, creating fantastic cakes. One took the shape of a train, complete with cargo and big wheels, another was a memorable narwhal with a horn that took up almost half the dining table, another a gingerbread house with a strawberry cake inside. I painted Easter eggs and sewed Halloween costumes. For Christmas we carved vegetable stamps and printed cards.

Raising children kept me sane, but my son grew up with a mother who barely knew how to word her own feelings. I wanted to find my own voice and to have some time off from child care and housework. I looked around for a daycare center, but there were few options in the early Seventies. Our first parent daycare co-op was dominated by a tyrannical man who chastised the parents at the weekly meeting. One toddler came to the group every day and bit all the children. Years later I found out the father used to beat this child all the time; the man was an alcoholic. The parent daycare co-op lasted for a year. For six months I sent my son to another daycare center. I knew it was not good, but I didn't have any choice .

Reading to my children at bedtime brought books and language back to my life. Every night my two-year-old son wanted to hear *The Little Engine That Could*. "I think I can, I think I can, I think I can. . ." became a mantra for both of us, struggling to climb the big hill of daily life. We went to the land of *The Cat in the Hat* and played with Thing One and Thing Two. Other nights became *Night Kitchen*: "I'm in the milk and milk is in me." We sailed one night and one year to *Where the Wild Things Are*. In *Nothing to Do* we learned how to rub a stone and find something to do. Hoban's Frances series taught us more about life, about childhood, than a big fat psychology book! My kids didn't realize that the children's books they took such delight in also helped me grow. Later we waded down the river into *Wind in the Willows* and traveled with Toad. All the nightly reading allowed me to invent a happier childhood and to become an American. We didn't have TV, a record player, or even a radio; we spent a lot of time going to the library. I was on welfare, with limited resources; books became our primary source of recreation and adventure.

When my daughter was four, I decided I was ready to do something about my body and the broken voice inside. Searching for an artistic community, I enrolled in a two-year training program in experimental theatre. The daily intensive training was partly based on Grotowsky's method, which called for rigorous body work and the purging of one's physical and emotional defenses, in order to learn to act spontaneously—to take risks without self-censorship. Pushing my stamina, learning gymnastic exercises, and going beyond my learned resistance made me get in touch with my body's strength, its unique way of recording and codifying my history. Deep bodywork uncovered memories lodged in the bone, the tangled web of nerves, the steady flow of blood. Each day was "keep stripping to the core," until I could feel the bone and its hollow places. Words, sounds started to resonate from my psyche, streams of images at first, and then fragments of long narratives sprouted from the darkest place of my memory. I read Anais Nin on the subway going home and late into the night. Her journey to become an artist made me feel I had only begun to merge my two halves into one: the dance of the Ying and Yang, earth and sky, the tiger and the dragon.

 As a girl I had the fearlessness of a hunter. I climbed the tallest tree in the neighborhood in Taipei, scaled brick walls. Going through the warm-up routines each day in the theatre loft, I marveled at the task before me. Like an archaeologist, I learned to examine every scrap of experience for knowledge, inspiration, and healing, to interpret the dragon bones' narrative, to connect with my former fearlessness. The sad part of the theatre school was that the majority of the students in the class remained strangers; there was no bonding, nor any resemblance to a community.

After two years of theatre training, I went for an audition. I was surprised when the director told me, "Li Min, you're talented, but you've got to find ways to stabilize yourself." Following this advice, I started tai chi classes and began to study the ancient texts of *feng shui* and the way of Tao.

In 1979, when my son was eight and my daughter five, a crazy man befriended by my partner was crashing in our basement and tried to fix a leaky pipe with a welding torch; he burned a hole in the wall, sending a flame to the attic. The nine-alarm fire torched our roof, damaging and destroying everything in the house. Firemen broke all the windows in the basement and first floor, and flooded all the rooms. Night river, night river, night river had taken away my art work, my books, my bed, roof, and floor. Our house was boarded up with plywood. Before Thanksgiving, a group of caring people came to help us bail water out of each room and clean up the wreckage. My dear friend Cindy made many trips to the laundromat to wash our smoke-filled clothes and bedding. Afterwards we gathered in the kitchen for a potluck Thanksgiving dinner. My partner and I took a shower together while our friends were setting the table. He asked me, "Should we go out to greet our friends naked?" He felt he had been born again.

That winter we put pots, pans, and buckets in different corners of the rooms to catch the leaks. Late one night I was awakened by the sound of dripping, the bing and bong from all the rooms, like an ancient Chinese water clock. I lay there breathing in the cold, listening to the bing-bong sound, the thawing of snow, the song of spring, surprised that I was not feeling depressed or run-down, like the fire-gutted house. Is it possible to become a drop of water? In each drop I discovered the moment; *to be here* is compassion.

Coda: My life is a vast ruin filled with stories. Here is a modern parable.

Green Dragon Sword

Liz Huaying Lee, nicknamed Tiger Girl, was a famous Hong Kong kung-fu movie star. After Liz won first prize in an International Sword Competition, her teacher, Sifu Chen, gave her the Green Dragon sword, a famous sword dating back to the Sung Dynasty. The eighteen-year-old was flattered, but a bit overwhelmed; she told Sifu that she was scared and maybe was not ready to receive the sword. To her amazement, old man Chen said, "You're ready, you don't have to wait any longer. You've mastered some of the hardest fighting forms and your body is superbly tempered, like the sword. But mostly it is your mind; it has finally calmed down to the perfect poise, being here with the tugging and flowing of Chi. We haven't had the luck to have a girl in the Chen family to dance with this sword. It's a male and I think it could use some of your female spirit. Dream of its origin; take a dream journey up the Shaman's Mountain, next to a great cliff where the purest spring flows.The forces of Ying and Yang wed there."

One afternoon, with the sword in her hand, Liz climbed to the top of Victoria Mountain and onto a small, flat, open space with a panoramic view of the sea on one side and the glittering lights of Hong Kong Island on the other. The blade was still cold after she tried out some of her moves, but within twenty minutes she felt at ease with it; she could pick out the dark and light, the ying and yang movements, until she and the sword became a spiral of energy. Coils of heat spun out from her movements and the sword became as flexible as a live serpent, hissing, undulating. Together they danced the spirit of Green Dragon.

As the shadows of the night sky thickened, her power grew. She focused on the sound she made, the lightness of her leaps, the silence of her footfalls, the rhythm of her breathing. The sword had its own eyes that watched for every fault, every weakness, while Liz ascended into the mountain's power. If she faltered, she would descend into the dark, blinding ground.

From the shadows of some nearby bushes, she saw an old man and an old woman waving short sticks with white horsetail whisks attached. Positioning themselves on either side of Liz, they dashed towards her. Without exchanging a word, they attacked, bronze blade versus horse hair, flesh versus spirits of masters. The opponents' Pa Kua Chuan, an internal fighting form, was so refined that the old couple created many illusions as they turned to encircle her. It was impossible for her to penetrate their monkey's triple somersaults, tiger's long leaps, snake's ground-spins. Their animal moves were gaining ground. Liz had never dreamt of encountering such an undefeatable pair. Their breathing was even throughout the combat, their eyes steely and focused. Just before she was going to get hurt by one of their wild moves, there would always be a warning sound like "Hey-ya!" Otherwise these master warriors spoke not a word. Her own movements became predictable. Her strength was ebbing; her breathing became uneven, and the sword felt cold and alienated.

The old man and old woman laughed and vanished, leaving just these words: "Go home, work harder on your kung-fu. We'll see you in ten years."

BLANCA BONILLA

ARRIVING

Moving to Boston was the most difficult challenge of my life. When I arrived, I could see from the taxi the big buildings, the lights everywhere, and the people on the sidewalk. It was July, very hot and humid. From the cab window I could feel the polluted air, not the same clean air I had been used to breathing. I felt like a stranger. My brother-in-law was talking to my father about all the good opportunities that we were going to have on the mainland and about cultural differences. "Gringos are crazy; all of them are hippies," he said.

We arrived at the Cathedral Projects where my sister Amelia lived. It was dark and the building was very tall. It was the biggest building I had ever seen. As we entered the hallway, we saw broken mailboxes and smelled urine. There were some black people in the hallway. We stared at them; they were speaking English and we did not know what they were saying. My brother-in-law told us right away that if we ignored them, they would not bother us. Once we went into my sister's apartment, there was a big difference; it was clean and neat. Four of us arrived that night. We had stayed on the island with my father, while my mother was already in Boston with the other children. We were together again.

We went to bed and the following morning we heard the train, the Orange Line. We all ran to the window to see it—it was like in the movies. After a couple of hours, we were homesick. I started crying and so did my sister Lucy and my brothers, Hector and Luis. We were feeling so sad.

A month later, we moved to our own apartment in Dorchester, and finally we made Jamaica Plain our home. I stopped living in the present, remembering my past and fantasizing a future in Puerto Rico. When I was home, I felt safe and happy. At school I did not like the food, the language, or the culture. I would sit in the back of the classroom just to be alone, so that I could have the space to daydream about the life I once had.

MARY MILLNER McCULLOUGH

IMBROGLIO

Settling back for the hour ride from O'Hare Airport to Michael Reese Hospital, Kela tried to relax after the bumpy flight from Los Angeles. As the taxi eased out onto the J. F. K. Expressway, she stared through the window to the pivotal moment, ten years ago, when her life had gone from predictable to precarious. Rev. Wright, a minister and her dad, had delivered a commandment she could not live by, so she packed two suitcases and left the home she had known for seventeen years. The ten dollars from her mom's purse was enough to get her from the East Side to the West Side. The words "Dumpling, you can come live with me anytime you want" carried her to her grandmother's house. She had waited until her mom and dad went to evening services. Kela could see the note left for her mom, fancy letters dancing above the lines on the paper, the fat loops on the r's and hollow circles dotting the i's. "Mom, Rev. Wright is not right this time. I am going to live with Grandma. I love you. Kela." *How young and foolish she had been.* When she fought with her parents as a child over her bedtime or over brushing her teeth, she had always threatened to run away to live with her grandmother. *Sticks and stones can break bones and words can cut you* hummed inside her head, competing with the memories surfacing from dusky waters.

The argument with her dad started when Peter brought her home at five in the morning. It was the second time she had come home past her eleven o'clock curfew. The first time she was late, her parents believed her when she told them that they had been talking in the car and lost track of time. The truth was that she had been rehearsing with Peter's band. When she tried to tell her dad the story about Peter's car running out of gas, he accused her of all sorts of lubricious behavior. It was so ludicrous she almost laughed at him, but stopped herself when his tone escalated into thunderous preaching.

"You are my daughter. I will not have you staying out until all hours of the night. What kind of reputation are you making for yourself? No respectable young woman comes home at five in the morning. Show some respect for me and your mother. The Bible tells us that the child shall honor the mother and father. How many more of the Lord's commandments have you broken? It's that boy's fault! I don't want you going out with that boy anymore. His kind is only interested in one thing!"

Kela's mom, always the peacemaker, tried to pacify him. "Now, Franklin, remember your blood pressure. Listen to what she has to say before you judge her."

But Dad, riding his own private roller coaster, started yelling about Peter and his kind.

Kela had thought she knew why her dad did not like Peter. She had invited Peter in to have a Coke. They were sitting in the kitchen when her dad walked across the yard from the church, through the back door. The house belonged to the church, but as long as Dad served as the minister, Kela's family lived in it rent-free. She had tried not to look at Peter through her dad's eyes. Peter was a tall, skinny, white boy with spiked black hair. His jeans had holes in them at the knees. Cleanliness being next to godliness, she knew her dad saw dirt. He wouldn't see the boy who was a great musician and a straight "A" student. Most of all, he would not see the boy who told her she was beautiful.

"Dad, this is Peter Salerno. He goes to the school of performing arts, same as me. He gave me a ride home."

Dad shook Peter's hand and thanked him, making it clear without saying it that he should leave.

"Where's your mother, Kela?" he asked her as Peter left the house.

"She went to the store. There's a note on the refrigerator."

"Do you think you should be entertaining when no one's in the house?"

"Don't be so old-fashioned, Dad. I'm fifteen," she asserted.

"How old is he?"

"He's a junior. I guess he's seventeen."

"Who's seventeen?" her mother asked as she came in the back door, carrying two shopping bags.

"Kela was entertaining a young man I think is too old for her," answered Dad.

"Who? Was it that young man from down the street who walked you home last week? He looked younger than Kela," her mom said, putting groceries away as she talked.

"No, this boy does not live down the street, unless a family moved in that I don't know about," her father said.

"We go to the same school. Peter lives in Centerville," she informed her parents. She dismissed the glance they exchanged.

"Centerville!"

"I know, Dad . . . the only city that you ever marched in where you questioned if God was really on your side . . . the only city where you doubted your faith . . . the only city where you learned what fear really felt like. Please. That was a long time ago."

"Things haven't changed, Kela. People who look like us still aren't safe in that city."

"Peter's not like those people."

"Aren't there some nice black boys in your school? I didn't march so my daughter could date a white boy from Centerville." His booming cadences began the Sixties history lesson that played like a drum in a duet with her heartbeat. Kela watched the large black man prancing and preaching across the kitchen floor. His arms like wings of a giant black bird shot up, his hands grew talons spewing fire. His words transformed into sound captured her, their meaning lost in the musical notes she started writing in her head.

"Your grandmother said I was asking for trouble when I told her I was organizing a march on Centerville. Why don't you save yourself the trouble and just throw a brick through the mayor's window, she told me. As the youth minister at the African Methodist Episcopal Church, I thought young people should get involved in the civil rights movement. We had a big planning meeting for all the young black people from as far away as Springfield. When we sang 'Ain't Nobody Gonna Turn Me 'Round,' I knew nothing was going to stop us. We had our prayer service early on that Sunday. Our sermon that day was our action, our march against hatred. Two hundred people came, mostly young men and women. We had hoped for more, but it was a good beginning.

"I was in front with Samuel Blues and Darnell Ware. We went down Main Street and turned onto Cougar Ave. Someone threw a rotten orange at us. We kept walking. That orange must have been some kind of signal, because the people lined up on either side of the street started throwing garbage at us. We sang louder. 'We Shall Overcome' became our battle hymn and our shield. I thought I heard a gunshot. Still we didn't slow down. Then everyone heard what sounded like machine gun fire. Ta-ta-ta-ta-tata. Panic, confusion, and fear took over. People started running over each other to get out of the way of death. I hit the ground. That's when I saw these white punks hanging out of a third story window, laughing. They had guns and were shooting into the air. The police who were supposed to protect us took just enough time to get there. Those cowards disappeared. Ten people ended up in the hospital that day, injured from falling or being stepped on. The leaders of the march, including your dad, were arrested for disturbing the peace."

Kela had auditioned to get into the school that drew talented students from all over Chicago. In the spring of her ninth grade year, she got the part of the Scarecrow in *The Wiz*. Peter, a junior, was one of the musicians in the band and arranged the music for the show. Kela had been singing all her life, in her father's church, and Peter loved music. He wrote songs about a white boy who loved an African lioness masquerading as a princess. Sometimes he would draw a picture of a rose on a piece of paper, and place her name in the center. She told him it wasn't easy being a minister's daughter, a model of goodness all the time.

She learned that his family thought of his music as a nice hobby. They expected him to grow out of it to become a mechanic or a priest. He told her he wanted to write beautiful songs for her to sing. By the end of her sophomore year, and Peter's senior year, they were in love. They went to Reed's Café and the Soho Lounge to listen to blues and jazz. Their favorite hangout was Mr. Jelly's, a crossover club on the North Side where black and white kids hung out together.

When Peter graduated from high school, he formed a band and spent most of his time writing and playing his electric guitar. He moved out of his parents' house to live above a cousin's auto repair garage. He made a little money working in the garage. Kela started singing with Peter's band. She rehearsed after school and told her dad different stories about school club meetings. They played for school dances to appreciative teenage audiences. Their heads filled with big dreams, and Peter started talking about heading west to California to try to sell some of his songs. She told him New York would be better because then they would be able to see each other.

Her parents made plans for her to go east to Howard University, their alma mater. They wanted her to get a good education just in case she didn't meet a nice black boy with a future to marry. She stopped going to choir practice and church. Dad threatened to send her to live with his mother in North Carolina. She threatened to move out and live with Peter.

Even her mom began to object. "He has too much influence on you, Kela. Your dad and I don't recognize our daughter any more. What happened to all the plans we made? You always wanted to go to Howard."

It was true. Peter had her thinking about other possibilities. She could sing and write songs too. She wanted the California sunshine. The lioness Peter knew announced to her parents, "I don't want to go to Howard." And the battle was on.

"I don't understand why you don't like Peter," she had yelled at her dad.

Mom reprimanded her, "Kela, don't speak to your father like that."

"Well, I don't understand. Why don't you try to get to know him?"

"I know him. I don't have to try to get to know him," her father answered. "He's like all the rest."

"Like the rest of who? Mom, what's he talking about?"

"It's because he's from Centerville," her mom explained.

"What's that got to do with his not liking Peter?"

And her father exploded, "I don't want my daughter going out with . . . with that white trash from Centerville."

Kela's heart fell to her knees. Minutes passed before she realized that she was holding her breath. She had listened to her father deliver sermons every Sunday about how people should treat others and how everybody was the same under the color of their skin. Good Christian values from the pulpit were repeated each day to her as she grew up. Kela went running after the little girl who loved her dad, begging her to come back. *Run around the house, catch a mouse; one, two, if I catch you, I'll put you in my shoe.* She wanted to make the words work the right way. Instead it all came out wrong. "I will see Peter whenever and wherever I want. You can't stop me."

"If you are going to live under my roof. . ."

She finished his sentence for him and yelled back, "I am living by YOUR rules! You're the one not living by your own damn rules."

For the first time in his life her father had hit her, and said the words that forced her out of the house: "If you can't abide by my rules in my house, then you can get out."

"Fine. I don't want to live with a bigot!"

When Rev. Wright and Mrs. Wright returned from evening prayer meeting, Kela was gone. She called Peter to tell him what had happened.

"It's all angry talk, Kela. It'll blow over by tomorrow."

"No, Peter. My dad's a hypocrite. You can reach me at my grandma's."

Mrs. Hairston, the church secretary, told Kela that she had found her number on the church phone Rolodex. She called to let her know her mom was in the hospital, in the intensive care unit at Michael Reese. They thought she'd had a heart attack. Then the secretary said, "Your dad wanted you to know."

Kela took the red-eye from L.A., praying that Mom was going to be all right. She had been trying to persuade her mom to come to California for a visit. Her mother kept saying she didn't want to fly, but Kela suspected she didn't want to visit without Dad coming along, and Kela had not invited him. Love for him had retreated to a corner, held under guard by the word bigot. Peter had become a symbol of her dad's hypocrisy. The real Peter went east before Kela graduated from high school. At first he wrote often to her about playing his guitar and living with friends in a loft. A few months before her graduation, the letters began to come less frequently. He called the morning of her graduation to say congratulations and share his news. He had met someone he liked a lot. *Baby, baby, she fell on the floor; baby, baby, don't cry any more.* Kela told him to send her a song, that she was headed west. She ended up working as a receptionist, going to school at night, and now was teaching music to children during the day and writing songs at night. She wrote to tell Peter she had sold her first song, but the letter came back stamped ADDRESSEE UNKNOWN.

The driver stopped at the entrance to the hospital. "This is it, Miss." The last time Kela had been here was to visit with her grandmother before she died. Not a happy memory to carry with her down the corridors and into the intensive care unit. At the desk, she told the nurse that she was Mrs. Wright's daughter.

"We moved her out of intensive care. Mrs. Wright is in

Room 22, one floor down."

Kela went to find the stairs and pushed open the door to Room 22. Her mom, brown skin stretched tightly over her small, fragile bones, was sitting up in bed, smiling. Dad stood near her on the right side of the bed. Kela took the left. "Kela, you didn't have to come all this way. I am fine. Just a little indigestion."

Kela leaned over to embrace her mom, giving her a kiss and a big smile, and held her, thinking, *She feels like she might just float away.* She looked up at her dad, who was staring towards the door.

"Dad."

"Kela."

"Mom, you look tired. Are you sure you are OK?"

"Nothing rest and some help won't cure," her dad answered.

The two-thousand-mile flight had taken her back ten years. Nothing had changed. *Right, Rev. Wright* went around and around in Kela's head. She heard these words when she was a ten-year-old standing by her dad's side as the congregation filed out of church to shake his hand after Sunday sermons. Sometimes members of the church called out during the sermon, "That's right!" Eventually the children created their own game, chasing each other with sticks, chanting, "*Right, right, Rev. Wright, when I catch you, you have to preach and shout.*" She liked the sound the words made, so every time her dad corrected her or solved her small childhood problems with scripture quotes, she would smile at him, happy that he was her father. She wrote her own praise song, *Right, Rev. Wright.*

Her mom's face pleaded. "Don't start, Franklin. She just got here." Then she asked Kela, "How long can you stay?"

"How long are you going to be in the hospital?"

"Oh, just a couple of days. Isn't that what the doctor said, Franklin?"

Kela looked at her dad, but he didn't reply. She wondered what he might be keeping from Mom. Looking closely at him, she saw lines on his face and worry in his eyes. His dark brown skin seemed mottled and discolored. He looked tired. The last time she had seen that worried face was when he came to Grandma's house to let Kela know she could come home. It was after his Sunday sermon. He started with how her mom was sad and that she should come back home because she owed it to her mother. Looking at him with her head turned to the side and one hand on her hip, she asked him, "If I come home, can Peter come over? Can I see Peter?"

"No. That just won't do, Kela."

"I guess I'll stay right here." Then she had gone upstairs to the room her grandma kept for her and slammed the door. No amount of talking from her mom and grandmother got either of them to forgive or forget. Her mom ended all her attempts at peacemaking mumbling to herself, "Two peas in a pod. Just two peas in a pod."

"Kela. Kela! How long can you stay?" Mom was asking.

"I have a whole week. I don't have to get back for a week."

"Good. We can have a good visit."

"Will you be staying at home?" her dad asked.

"Yes."

The idea of staying there with Dad until her mom came home did not appeal to her. She tried to remember that she was no longer a little girl.

"That'll be fine. I'll take your bag to the car." Dad took the bag from the chair where she had placed it and walked out of the door. "I'll wait for you in the car. I'll see you in the afternoon, Lillian. You rest now."

Her mom breathed a sigh of relief. "Kela, try to understand your dad. He's trying. You have to try. I can't keep trying to fill that empty space between the two of you. It's wearing me out."

"All these years, he hasn't had much to say to me."

"He doesn't know how to talk to you."

"He talks to people all the time. He knows how."

"But he doesn't know how to talk to you. He's a little afraid of you. Has been ever since you started having ideas of your own, good courageous ideas of your own. Kela, he's under a lot of pressure right now. He's been working with some other ministers and priests to organize a thirtieth anniversary march through Centerville. He's been working to involve the young men from Centerville in the planning. I think he's doing this for you."

"It's not the Sixties any more."

"Did you hear what I said? He's doing this for you."

"When is all of this supposed to take place?"

"After Sunday's interfaith service at the church. The planning has been going on for months. I think there's a final meeting tonight. Why don't you go? See for yourself. I think you'll be proud of your dad."

"For you, I'll go."

As Kela walked from the house to the church, she could hear the music and noise of people gathering for the evening's meeting. She positioned herself on the end of a pew, where she had a clear view of what was happening at the front of the church, but where she could leave without being noticed. The church was filling up. Extra chairs had been set up in a row facing the congregation. There were brown, black, and white faces sitting side by side, talking with each other as they waited. Several men and a woman huddled near the pulpit. A group of young men entered with her father, from his office. She recognized a couple of them as the boys, now grown, who had teased her in Sunday School. But her attention was riveted on a tall, skinny, white young man closing the office door. He looked disheveled, in his leather jacket and torn blue jeans. His hair, spiked down the center of his head, was purple and green. What on earth is that, she thought, looking at the young man with her father's eyes. Rev. Wright's extended hand froze in an incomplete handshake. A sound like a kite being blown away by March winds sliced the hot air around her. Her father's arms had suddenly stretched out like an accordion fan, to re-fold swallowing up every inch of the boy's upper torso. All she could see were protruding green tips like needles from a pin cushion. Kela moved forward to watch the drama unfolding at the pulpit. Rev. Wright released Green Tips to the choir on his right. Where did he get these people? They don't belong in the choir. Kela remembered a choir filled with black women and men who sang spirituals and called out Amen in response to her dad's sermons. This choir looked like mud cloth.

Rev. Wright stepped to the podium. "Before we start tonight, I'd like to introduce you to a special visitor who is here all the way from Los Angeles. My daughter, my joy, Kela Wright."

Kela stood. Embarrassed by the eyes and heads turned in her direction, she stepped into the aisle, preparing to leave by the nearest exit. Sensing her imminent retreat, Rev. Wright descended from the pulpit as if he had stepped on a fast-moving escalator going down. He stopped when he reached the floor and looked over the heads towards Kela. His long arms hung from drooping shoulders. His eyes squinted and twitched, while his hands floated up and then down, trying to find a resting place. Her dad seemed shorter, fragile. Opening his mouth as if to begin a prayer, he raised his face to the faded heavens painted on the ceiling.

"God. You know that I am not always right, but I am not a

bigot." Everyone stared through the silence at Rev. Wright. His roaring cry echoed down from the pinnacle of the roof. He tried to speak. "I ask . . . I ask. I ask under . . ."

Kela watched as he clutched at the sleeves of his robe, indiscernible words gurgling in his throat. He seemed to be sinking. She ran to his side, thinking he was having a heart attack. Placing her hand gently on his right shoulder, she watched him open his eyes and look at her. His back straightened and his chest inflated as if being filled by helium. "Forgiveness, I ask for your forgiveness," he said. Then he turned to the organist behind him and nodded. And the new choir began to sing, "*Shall we gather at the river, the beautiful, beautiful river.*"

Elena Harap

APRIL 1968

It was April and Martin Luther King had been killed. New England's spring was cold and raw. My nine-month-old son, suffering with an earache, cried and cried. Remembering that my husband Ted had been at the March on Washington, my mother-in-law called to tell us the news. Ted cried too. The doctor made a house call, an unusual service in Boston. The house was draped with damp laundry; our clothes dryer had broken down, an added misery for the baby. I had washed his favorite blanket and now it was a sodden, heavy lump of wool. I tried to iron it dry so that he could hold it.

There was no comfort for the people who loved and followed Dr. King. I went to my job at a Roxbury settlement house; a teenager paced the halls aimlessly—his face a frown of pain, his conked hair wrapped in a doo rag, saying, "They killed my leader." The air was full of tension and when we heard reports of looting and vandalism on Blue Hill Avenue, my co-worker Mary Goode said quietly, "Elena, I think you better go home." I felt as never before how I was white, not relevant here. My very presence put everybody at risk. There was no hostility in Mary's eyes, only a sober acceptance that this moment had to be faced within the family of the black community. As I went home to my neighborhood of Mission Hill, only a few streets over, a curtain seemed to close behind me; and behind the curtain I sensed a watchful gathering and an intimate, fathomless mourning.

The baby's ear infection healed and he smiled again. The streets of Roxbury became quiet and I went back to my job. Money poured in for programs, yet Boston's denial of adequate education, decent jobs and housing, cultural equality, and a political voice to its black citizens had barely begun to be addressed. During the years that followed, in a divided city we all had to try to find the meaning of King's example for ourselves. School busing plunged neighborhoods into violent crisis; parents learned to advocate for their own and others' kids, while others opted out; colleges formed African-American studies programs and later neglected them; Martin Luther King's birthday became a national day of remembrance. In Vermont, where I now live, in the 1990s it is the same: the work, learning, and celebration go on. And still when I recall the day King died, I hear the sad, insistent sound of my son's crying.

PRACTICE WHAT YOU PREACH

I am standing in front of the mirror, fixing my dress. As he walks into the bedroom, I see him through the mirror. He has a slight smile on his face, forming two big peaches on his cheeks. His blue eyes open wide as he looks me up and down. I turn around to face him; at the same time I am trying to fix my hair. He stands in front of the door, straight as a soldier, with shoulders as wide as a football player's. He is moving slowly towards me. With a very deep voice he says, "You are not going out like that!" I smile and turn to the mirror to brush my hair. This is not the first time I have heard this statement.

"People might think you are easy," he continues. "If I were you, I would be cautious of the clothing I wear."

"Well, Ramón," I respond, "you shouldn't be concerned about what people think about you. You know who you are. People think what they want anyway."

He does not allow me to support my statement. "That is not what you say when I wear my crazy clothes." He moves closer toward me and very gently tugs down my dress, trying to make it longer. We smile at each other. He moves away from me, lies down on the bed, and says, "Mom . . . you should practice what you preach."

MARY MILLNER MCCULLOUGH

IN THE WILDERNESS

i am incomplete
a firefly flashing
on off
in the night sky
a June beetle
on a journey to explore
burning up
my wings tied to a child's string
straining to soar
certain that my bug status
is temporary

The swallowtail butterfly drinks nectar from the hibiscus flowers at the edge of my yard and moves on. Unlike me, it does not need to examine each petal of the flower or compare and contrast the sweetness of the nectar. Butterfly. It is free. It lives in a clearing of sorts, gathering substance as it travels from one bloom to another. Me. I was born in a wilderness, and although there is beauty and food here, I want the clearing. So I seek the beacon that lights the path through the brambles. Birth.

> *I don't know the whole story*
> *only bits and pieces*
> *so how can I begin in the beginning*
> *I must trust the dream world*
> *I was born in a room that had been darkened to receive me*
> *I shot from a woman's body, face down*
> *but I quickly raised my head and gave a good strong yell*
> *I landed in the hands of my aunties, who cried out,*
> *"What's the rush, child? Hold your horses,*
> *and wait until we are ready."*
> *The sisters shook their heads and sucked their teeth*
> *This was my first lesson in how to show disapproval*
> *although I must confess*
> *I did not perfect the technique until*
> *I had children of my own.*

I was born in May, a daughter of spring and grand-daughter of miscegenation, a great-grand-daughter of Europe's rape of Africa and victimizing of the peoples of the Americas. I was born at the end of farming, just in time to learn the importance of planting a garden. I watched people who loved the feel of dirt in their hands go to work in factories. I longed for my older cousins who migrated to big cities in search of a better life.

I grew up in a black community in southwest Virginia, determined to ignore the signs that read "For Colored Only." Against the background of the Ku Klux Klan, Jim Crow laws, institutionalized and legal segregation, internalized racism and sexism, and a family trying to survive, I was born leaving. Looking back, I can see the natural beauty of the town I lived in, located in the foothills of the Blue Ridge Mountains. As a child, I saw only the beauty of those creatures who could fly away. Flight seemed the only way out. I lived in fear.

I was the first child of Nannie and Frank Millner. My father was a hunter and fisherman, my mother a homemaker and Bible reader; both were workers. I learned to skin a rabbit, pluck chickens, shoot a gun, to fish, to love Bible stories, and to crochet chains of lace. Adults often said, "Do as I say do, not as I do." It was confusing, making no sense.

My mother and father's circumstances did not poison their parenting. My sister, brother, and I were expected to behave respectfully towards every person, no matter what color, to work hard, and always to do our best. They tried to teach me not to judge individuals, or to hate southern white folks, and at the same time would not let me play with children who were not blood relatives. There were plenty of cousins to pick as playmates. I did not have friends outside the family until I went to high school. I became friends with girls who looked white. They were so white-looking that if they had lived in the white community, I could not have told that they were black. Talk about people's skin color was rampant and ruled who associated with whom. My family and community included people of every possible shade of brown, from ebony to almond. My parents didn't have any difficulty accepting my choices until, as a teenage girl, my eyes lingered too long on a boy of ebony hue named Hezekiah.

> . . . *Talk from the family*
> TOO BLACK
> *Taboo*
> *for our yellow girl.*

Too late
what they said.
yellow girl
fell in love
with his black skin
his white teeth
his sweetness
his grin.

Fell in love
with his name
Hezekiah. Hezekiah.

The world outside my community delivered a powerful message about who I was supposed to be. It said, *You are colored. Your role in this world is to serve us. You are inferior to us, not as smart, and cannot follow any path that takes you away from the role we have assigned you.* My family and community, having received their own messages, said, *You are a girl. You can be smart but not as smart as boys. You are to help your mother, clean and cook, serve and take care of the men. Get an education, work and support yourself until you find a husband who can support you. Be his helper. Be submissive.* The war was on. A voice summoned me to the battle. *Black, black girl. Where you be, where you be!* I answered, *I be trying to integrate these two pieces of me.* Black and female.

The sisters stood on either side of the bed
consoling my mother for what was to come
A female is born.

As I observed men's behavior toward women, I surmised that colored men were the bosses in their homes, even if white men ruled them beyond their front doors. Women worked harder than men, leading messier lives with all the cleaning, cooking, sewing, children, and taking care of the sick. Women seemed less powerful to me, less in charge of what I thought really mattered, which was the freedom of coming and going as you pleased. That is what my dad could do. I preferred the life my father led outside the house, even though I didn't know anything about it. He drove the car, my mom drove the broom; so I rebelled at homemaking. When I was supposed to make beds, sweep floors, or do dishes, I would stop, as soon as no one was looking, to read comic books. I yearned for superpowers like Superman and Plastic Man. I slipped into their adventures.

> 1943: *a sister is born who tries to bite me out of existence*
> *Dad is in the Philippines*
> *male influences are gone*
> *to fight the Japanese and the Germans*
> *women rule quite nicely*
> *life seems gentler*
> *against clicking sounds and warm hands*

Excuses were not acceptable, nor was lying or stealing. I took money from my mom's purse once and lied about it. Lying was something I practiced to see if I could do it. When mom found me out, she said that she would tell my dad when he got home. I waited anxiously for my punishment and the four o'clock factory whistle, signaling that another work day had ended. Would I be sent to find the switch which would leave red welts on the backs of my legs? It took a long time to figure out it was best to tell the truth. The punishment for lying was always worse than the punishment for the original misdeed.

When I was about three years old, we moved to our own house. It was located on the corner of Bethel Lane and Williams Street in East Martinsville, a colored section of Martinsville, Virginia. It became a famous place on a winter afternoon in 1949 when a white woman was allegedly raped by a "gang" of seven black men ranging in age from seventeen to thirty-seven. The men were tried and all seven were found guilty and sentenced to death in the electric chair. The pursuant protests, both legal and otherwise, did not result in a stay of execution. On Feb. 2, 1951, four of the seven were electrocuted. Three days later, the remaining three met the same fate. Someone wrote in a newspaper that "never before in Virginia had that many men been executed at the same time." I was nine years old when the tragedy took place, and fear came to live with me as my constant companion.

A vacuum sucked their souls away before their bodies died and mourned their loss by stealing the songs of the birds of winter. That is how it seemed to me as my feet hit the frozen dirt road that I walked home each day from school. I couldn't feel the warmth of the bright sun. Something awful had happened. I was aware of brightness in a barren landscape, a place without life, without air. *Where is everybody?* I wondered. I was answered by a silent "hant." *Hant* is the word my grandfather used for *ghost* in the stories he told at twilight time on his porch in the summer months. One landed on my back that day. Its intention, I thought, was to use me to take back its human form. I stood firm and did not struggle. My grandfather's hants were always jumping on somebody's back, trying to get something back that had been taken from them. One had hold of me that afternoon in 1949. It shook my whole body, but to others it appeared that I had the trembles. When my parents asked if I felt all right at the supper table that night, I said that I felt fine. I knew that the hant was causing the shaking, but my parents couldn't see it. They told me to stop, but when they realized that I couldn't stop it, even under their orders, I was taken the next day to see the doctor. He told them, "Nothing wrong with her that I can see." I knew that he couldn't see it. I lived with that hant for three whole days and three nights. I watched it and hummed to myself as I waited to see what it would do. It left me quietly and without fanfare on the fourth morning.

Although I was about the best nine-year-old eavesdropper you are ever likely to meet, I was never successful in hearing any adults discuss the Martinsville Seven, or the alleged rape and the trial that led to their execution. My child's space in the world, full of wonders and horrors, did not collide with theirs. With one of my male cousins, I talked about the unfair justice system for colored men. We vowed that when we grew up, we would find justice for those seven men. We knew they were innocent. "I am going to become a lawyer," he declared. "And I will write the story," I told him. Our pact to right wrongs provided me with a feeling of belonging and a shared purpose.

Our square house had a living room used for company on Sundays and afternoon siestas in hot summer months. It was heated by an oil-burning stove in the winter, but the stove was lit only on Sunday for guests. Most of the time the room was closed off so that it would not suck the heat from the rest of the house. My parents' bedroom was next to the living room for a short while, but later their bedroom became a dining room and they put up two walls with a door in the attic, where we all slept. The stairs from the attic went down into a kitchen with a wood cook stove, and next to the kitchen was a sitting room where we did homework and played games. A TV set was added when I was eleven years old. Our indoor plumbing didn't work well, so we kept our outhouse clean. I liked the privacy of the outdoor privy. The indoor toilet was filled with the scent of my parents.

I spent as much time as I could out-of-doors. I liked the world of flying things and spent many long hours watching hummingbirds and listening to the cries of buzzards. I wondered what dead things they had found to eat. When I became hungry, I would snatch green peaches and apples from trees and gobble them down with pinches of salt stolen from the kitchen.

Relatives surrounded us. Mom's sisters lived on the same street, with their husbands and children. My fathers' parents lived a stone's throw from my back yard. Most of the people in the small community lived off the land. Some women worked as maids. Some worked in the factories beside the men. Older people, like my grandparents, made their way in the world the best way that they could. Everyone had a garden and many raised pigs and chickens. Sometimes we traded green beans for beef. Game was plentiful and Mom cooked whatever my father killed in the woods. If I had to help with the skinning or killing, I couldn't eat the meat. I liked the dumplings, gravy, and vegetables, but would say "No, thank you", to the rest. My bones grew on the nutrients of evaporated milk sweetened with sugar and kept in an icebox. I was happy. I left my yard to play next door with my cousins, left on their own while my Aunt Tilly went to take care of white folks' kids. My dad came home earlier than usual one day and found me playing in my cousins' yard. His switching did no good. It just taught me to get home from my forbidden wanderings before he returned. A house with ten children in charge of themselves was too good to miss.

My mother's mother owned a seventy-eight-acre farm where she managed the growing of tobacco, peanuts, guinea hens, a few mules, cows, and her seventeen farmhand children. We drove to see her on Sundays. I have one snapshot of myself running in the grass outside her log cabin. I look about three years old. Grandma Witcher liked me. Her parents were Indians; Mom constantly told us that we were Cherokees and talked about her grandfather, who made beads and skirts for her and her sister Matilda. She said that Indians had their own schools. Mom attended the colored school. She and Matilda wore their beads and were made fun of by the other students. It must have been painful for her and her sister. Mom said that one day, on the way home, they took the beads off and threw them into the woods. In a dream once, I asked my mother, "How do you know who you are?" She looked at me and said, "Education has made you stupid" and proceeded to tell me stories that ended with, "We're Cherokee, you know." Who I am spills out of me in my writing.

In the garden, my parents taught their children lessons about life. Seeds ordered in the winter months would be put into the soil in early spring. Plants were rotated so that the nutrients of the soil wouldn't be used up. Certain plants could grow together and others had to be separated. Soil around the plants had to be tilled so that the roots could breathe, weeds had to be pulled. The garden lessons were my dad's proudest moments. His father had been a tenant farmer and he knew a lot about potatoes. Dad and Granddad gladly shared their knowledge with anyone willing to listen. Dad told us many times that he had to work on the farm and that his dad did not allow him to go to school.

After supper each evening, we walked to my grandparents' house to sit on their front porch. Grandpa would tell stories or discuss the Bible with my mom. They would argue about certain points of interpretation of the scriptures. Grandpa was a Primitive Baptist minister who enjoyed preaching and talking as much as I liked looking and listening.

"YOU MUST STAY IN THE LINES OR YOU'LL LOSE." Coloring books and obedience were the main activities at home. The coloring prepared me for penmanship and following directions. Obeying my parents meant that I would listen to other adults, like my teachers, or be beaten with a stick. The coloring books in my house always had a sentence under each picture and a clue about what colors things should be on the page. *Mary wears a red dress when she waters the yellow buttercups.* Sometimes in the evening, my dad would color with us or teach us a card game. His picture was always colored the best, and he never lost a card game. He competed with us, using tricks and cheating at the card games. He laughed as he boasted about how he won all the time. I think we were supposed to figure out the tricks and take on the challenge of attempting to get the best of him. By eleven I participated less and less in his games. Looking up from my school books when my dad, sister, and brother were engaged in card games Dad called "Tonk" and "Cooncane," I kept to myself the knowledge that my sister and brother would never win.

At six years old, in the fall of 1946, I left home and the comfort of days spent with my mom, to go to grade school. I walked to school in a group of children, wearing a new dress made from blue-flowered cotton feed sacks. My sister cried to go with me, but she would have to wait three years before it was her turn.

I distinctly remember my first days of school as ones of challenge. The school was a one-story, red-brick structure, about two miles from my home. I walked with the other children through a poor, working-class, white community to get to school. The building sat at the edge of a lot. There was a play area for recess that eventually was paved over. Right before Christmas, during one recess, the principal threw bright red apples from his office window to the students below on the ground. I did not realize at the time that we were considered poor. Someone had donated apples to the poor children at the black school, and the principal threw them to us from his window. I look for that taste each time I bite into an apple even now.

Except for the school building, the play area seemed like an empty lot. Wooden-frame homes faced the school on two sides; a road and a street bordered the other sides. The street had more houses, and across the road was a large gully, beyond which ran a major rural route that divided the white and black neighborhoods. The road was dangerous to cross. There were no crossing guards, and like every other young person, I just looked both ways, took my chances, and ran across.

The school was divided into four rooms. Two rooms on one side of the building were for children in grades one through three, and the other two, separated by a partition which could fold back, making one large room, were for fourth through sixth grades. Fifth graders attended in the afternoon shift. One teacher taught fourth and fifth grades. Once you successfully negotiated sixth grade, you could walk or ride the public bus across town to another black community for grades seven through twelve. To get there, I again had to pass through the white community, which always seemed to be located centrally, with smaller "colored" communities just outside its boundaries. I could have avoided the white town altogether by walking though the woods. I did that once, but did not try it again for two reasons. It was not interesting to me; I liked seeing people and houses. And somewhere, in the deeper recesses of my brain, I knew the woods were dangerous for a young colored girl.

My first lesson was not fun. The teacher, having written the alphabet across the top of the chalkboard in capital and small letters, proceeded to call on students to identify the letters. My classmates answered correctly. When it was my turn to recite what I had come to school to learn, I was unable to answer, since the teacher had not taught it to me yet. It was humiliating. I went home that day feeling as if the world had become a little less trustworthy. I later learned that many of the students in the first grade had gone to something called "kindergarten," where they had been prepared for first grade. My perceived failure on the first day made me mad. I became determined to prove myself worthy and never to be embarrassed in a classroom of peers again. Achieving that goal during my first years of school meant that I wouldn't take risks if it meant that I might be wrong. I lost the confidence that I brought to school. I had to figure out how to get it back. I knew that if I worked hard, I would eventually know the letters like everyone else. Within a week, I knew all of my letters and letter sounds and was on my way to reading, along with all those kindergarten-attending students. The other lesson I learned was about social class and how it plays a pivotal role in school success. I was always trying to prove to those same "colored" students who had opportunities unavailable to me that I was just as good as they were.

Sitting at my desk in fourth grade, I found out quickly what the white society in the town expected of me. The message was communicated through a white woman who entered our classroom with a wooden box which had holes in it. Each child got a turn at putting different-size pegs into slots in the box. I wasn't very good at it. I can remember sitting at my desk struggling to understand the point of what I was being asked to do. "You'll be good at factory work," said the white woman, when I finished my turn at the box. It turned out to be a ridiculous aptitude test where all of the "colored" students were in learning circumstances that placed them at a disadvantage.

Colored teachers reinforced the same values as my family and the community people, who seemed to be interested in helping steer me along their right path. Reminders about how I should be in the world came in the form of a look, a word, or a stick, if I was having a difficult time learning my lessons. Parents were always told how their children behaved. The teachers were black women who looked white, with the exception of the third grade teacher, Mrs. Starling. She was a black lady with brown skin. I did not know then that I would not have teachers who looked like me across the "Mason-Dixie" Line. I am fortunate because I have the memory of my teachers' caring about their students and being able to show it. All students should have the same opportunity, especially students of color.

The elementary school principal was Rev. Anderson, a highly respected and stern minister in the community. An identified leader by blacks and whites, he ruled the school with two sticks, and was the boss over the women teachers. His treatment of female students differed only in that the smaller stick was reserved for girls who did not behave. He taught the sixth graders and dished out the punishment to those sent to his office. I was afraid of him and don't remember learning much in his class, except to be quiet. His classroom was crowded with students squeezed by two's into one seat. My first opportunity to participate in a writing contest, sponsored by Westinghouse, came in sixth grade, in his class. Sixth graders were chosen by the teacher to write an essay on what our dads meant to us. I think I was selected because I was obedient. I wrote that my dad was important to me because he bought me things. I filled pages with a list of those things. I knew as soon as I turned my paper in that it had no substance and conveyed nothing abut how I felt about my dad. I don't think I could have expressed how I felt about any member of my family in sixth grade.

> . . . To reveal self is risky at best but to reveal self to those who
> will judge the revealing is sure terror. It's like falling into empty
> space from a great distance, flapping your arms and legs,
> screaming, because you have no parachute . . . .
> (from my journal, July 1997)

Feelings expressed could get you into serious trouble, so I swam on the surface of life where I knew it was safe. Not winning was the best lesson about writing that I received in grammar school. The winner's essay was read to the class. It was very good writing by a female student who lived near the school on a dirt road that got washed away when it rained. After hearing her essay, I walked with her home after school, to see her house and to feel her life at home. I sent the pictures of what my eyes saw to my brain. She must have thought I was strange. We had not spoken before, and once I had my pictures, she faded into the background again.

Writing was not about forming neat, perfect letters evenly spaced on lines, or single words listed with commas or grammatically correct sentences, or spelling. Writing was much more than that, and someone who was not an A student won the contest and received the praise. This happened more than once in my schooling. One of the best writers that I knew in high school was a C student, a young woman we called Pinky, who dropped out of school in the eleventh grade. I think she was pregnant. That's what she had written about in English class. She wrote about her real life experience and a condition for which I silently condemned her. Her writing was good even if, at that time, I thought she was not. Even now, the fact that I considered the writing good seems more important than anything else I might have thought at the time.

"Your mom read to you all the time," said my dad, "don't you remember?"

My memories of learning to read and write are vague. The experiences of schooling are vivid. Being teased, bullied, chased on the way home by a dog belonging to a red-headed white girl who said, "Sic that nigger," recess and stick ball games, and crushes on boys are the things I remember clearly about school. I remember the word "nigger" and the dog chasing me each day after school. The classroom and lessons from teachers are as obscure and blurred as the image of Mom reading to me. I write to rid myself of fear.

I didn't choose to step into your life
you forced me across the distance
burned labels into me with your English words
built a canal though my heart
castrated my sons violated my daughters
fashioned your stories by omission
and unauthorized absence
Now I am going to write the stories so I can save myself.
Because I'm
going out of my mind
'bout this race thing
give you all I'd got
just for some peace and quiet
white people
Make a space for me   inside your head
cause I'd gotta know   gotta know
what 's like, what is it like
What IS IT LIKE to be free?

The first book I remember getting in school that held my interest and was mine to keep would be called a literature book today. My parents paid for it and my other school books with money saved during the summer months. The day we received our new books was one of the most exciting days at school. I carried mine home in a new book satchel. At home, I would hold each book in my hand, looking at its cover before turning its pages. I would go through each book, looking at all the lessons we would have for the school year. I can still clearly see some of the illustrations that accompanied the stories in my first real literature book.

I remember the story I read of a farm family in a place called Iowa. They grew corn, storing it in a barn. A young girl, portrayed as not too smart, accidentally started the stored corn popping and it rained down like snow, covering the entire farm. Other stories were more like folk tales. One favorite was about a competition between Summer and Winter, in which the two attempted to get a man to remove his coat. The harder Winter worked, blowing cold winds, the tighter the man pulled his coat around him. All Summer had to do was to let the sun shine hotter and hotter. The only story I ever read about Native Americans in my childhood was in that book. It was the story of five Native American children who disobeyed their parents by going to dance in the woods. They never came out because they danced until they became a long string of stars in the night sky.

Unfortunately, I read all the stories in one week. Nothing was left and even though I would look at the pictures again, I didn't re-read the stories. Our school did not have a library, so I turned back to my comic books. The practice of buying books for students to keep changed. We were given used books, outdated and passed on to us from white schools.

At home we had a few books that my mom read. One was about someone called Lorna Doone and another was titled *Rebecca*. I flipped the pages, looking for words and pictures that would capture my interest. Mom's books did not have any. The large, worn Bible, with recorded births in it, had beautiful religious drawings of Jesus Christ and his disciples. The colors were oranges, yellows, browns, and reds. Each illustration was covered with thin, tissue-like paper that allowed the picture beneath to appear like a ghost on a page. When the tissue paper was lifted, a vibrant painting appeared. I have often wondered what happened to that Bible.

A most wondrous present was given to me one Christmas Day. It was a new book, *The Five Little Peppers*. The book told the story of five children in the Pepper family. Like a child licking an ice cream cone, trying to make it last, I read in spurts, but by the next afternoon, it was finished. I was driven by a hunger. I used to think it was because I did not have enough to eat; and I thought that my memories of eating green fruit and red dirt might have been related to physical hunger or to a kind of vitamin deficiency. I am not so sure anymore. If I could go back to mentor the child who was me, I would take books.

In seventh grade, on one of those rare days when I walked home from the school I attended across town without Lucy, my constant companion to and from school, I looked up to see a library directly across the street from me. I knew what was inside. That night at the dinner table I announced to my parents that I planned to go into the library the next day to take a look at some books. They knew and I knew that the library, although public, was part of the Jim Crow system, off-limits to little colored girls.

The next day I stood on the sidewalk across from the library and stared. My school did have a library, but after being unable to go into the forbidden library, I lost interest in exploring what was there. When I returned home from my first year at college—and after my sister and other students had held their sit-in at the Woolworth counter without incident—I made a trip to the segregated library of my past. At first I found it hard to breathe as I walked slowly around the very small space, waiting for someone to tell me that I couldn't be there. Nothing happened. I went to the shelves, examining the books, looking for what it was all about. I found a book about the relationships of blacks and Indians in the South, entitled something like *Black and Red Together*. I took it to a sunny table in a corner near a window to read. The place was pleasant. The people there were pleasant. It was an interesting book which I have not run into anywhere else, but the one-story building that was like forbidden fruit to a young colored student in 1952 no longer met my taste standards. I rejected it and have never gone back.

I started school knowing jump rope rhymes. I knew clapping games from the aunt who lived with us and from playing with my cousins. I loved Bible stories from the Old Testament. It is very possible that these were my first stories. How did I become literate? My parents, who were wise if unschooled, prepared me for the challenges of learning. My mom could read and enjoyed it. She shared it with me. She had learned, even though she had only completed the sixth grade. My dad, a smart man, often says, "If only I had your education, I could have gone far in this world." My desire to attain knowledge, my need to understand, and the encouragement of black teachers did the rest. Teachers are powerful. They can nurture and help you until you can do it on your own. They can also destroy that one vital human ingredient necessary for survival, spirit.

In fifth grade I made a decision that helped me move beyond the role of silent spectator to one of comic mimic. For some reason that isn't clear even to me, I volunteered to perform on the spot in front of my classmates, when the teacher asked students to entertain the class. I don't have the vaguest notion of what the lesson was about that day. I just know that I volunteered. My observant self warred with the self who had volunteered. I waited as others went up to sing or recite a poem before the class. I had no idea what I would do. Again that quirk that often gets me into trouble was operating. I knew, whatever it would be, that I could do it. My turn came. I left my seat and went to the front of the class. I looked at faces waiting in expectation, opened my mouth, and out came Nat King Cole singing "Answer Me, Oh My Love." It sounded just like him to me—and to those fifth graders too. I got a round of applause from my peers and a big smile from the teacher. When I finished, I did not sit down. I went immediately into an imitation of Marilyn Monroe, which got a lot of great laughs from the class and a "Thank you, Mary. You may sit down," from the teacher. I liked the attention from the audience and auditioned for parts in plays in high school and college. I got a few in college, as I studied theatre arts, but I never got a part in high school. Maybe I wasn't good enough, but I suspect that the "wrong" part of town was operating, since the main parts always went to those kids who had gone to kindergarten. I wrote some comic bits for talent shows, which the audience loved. Making people in an audience laugh had to substitute for a part in Pride and Prejudice. Performing what I wrote seemed to be the only way I was going to get on stage, so that's what I did whenever the opportunity presented itself. It all started back in fifth grade.

The older I get, the more important and urgent is the need to write. Writing makes me aware of living. It is a process that incorporates memories of pain, joy, laughing-out-loud sounds, and terrors. When I write, the visions are as clear as the diamonds that stay in store windows. Sometimes the tears come back and sometimes I laugh. My difficulties come when I know what I wish to tell the reader, or suggest, or keep secret, and am unable to find the words that will do justice to my images. Therein lies my struggle.

One creative writing piece, an English assignment in high school, was about my brother Frank. When he was born, I thought that he was a miracle. Shortly after his birth, my mom had a nervous breakdown and was hospitalized. I was eight years old and in the third grade. My sister was five. Dad took care of all of us. I would watch him playing with my baby brother through a crack in the door that separated the kitchen from my parents' bedroom. It was fun to look at the two of them when he didn't know that I was watching. My brother, as he grew up, developed a forlorn look that made his face appear elongated. Sometimes he was funny. I wrote about his antics and misadventures. He was caught playing with matches several times, and although he was told about the danger, he continued to flirt with fire until he managed to get a major conflagration started. In my story I told how he set a whole field on fire. I described the grass blazing away and the three of us trying to put it out. There was humor in the event. It did not have a tragic ending, except the unfortunate circumstance of my dad coming upon us as we battled the mighty forest fire Frank's fire had become in my story. The first draft was exciting and funny, and the energy of it was felt by the teacher; it made her laugh. Then she asked me to do a second draft. I didn't understand. I thought that I was done. I tried to do what she told me. As I reworked the product, it didn't get better, it just got dull and boring, a little like the essay I wrote in sixth grade.

The real work of writing is not when you put the first words down, but when you take the first draft that is the diamond in the rough and make it shine through rewriting. As the stick I selected for my own whipping had to sing when flexed against the air, words that I choose must hum in rhythm to the beat inside my head. The more literate I become, the clearer the song I choose to sing.

To let the writing go where it needs to go, I must take the risk to reveal myself, share strong emotions, good and bad. In the writing of these pages, I came to the realization that all writing is about self. There is no way to escape. The struggle is in gaining control over it, finding one's voice, and choosing to tell the story.

I want to write about ordinary people with extraordinary notes. I want my students to learn to write about what is important to them, to find their authentic selves and ways of being in the world, and to learn about their courage through taking the risks to tell their stories. Writing can do that for students.

I think living is a great courageous act we commit each time we rise to meet a new day. There are other bold deeds, carried out by individuals and by whole groups of people. Most African captives chose life in their new worlds. I want their hope to find its way into the stories children read in school. This is beginning to happen in some schools. I want all people of color to have the opportunity to read stories about themselves as heroes and heroines, as people with tremendous grit and gifts to give the world. I want to take commonplace, taken-for-granted events, and through a creative process and use of my writing craft, to stimulate and inspire these kinds of stories. I knew so many brave people, growing up as a young girl in the South. Their stories, if told well, will keep their spirit and mine alive forever. I will be as honest as I can be. That's the only promise a really good liar can make.

BLANCA BONILLA

COSAS DE LA NOCHE/
THINGS OF THE NIGHT

Mi madre tenía solamente quince años cuando se casó con mi padre que tenía cuarenta y un años. Un año después tuvieron su primera hija, Amelia, nació en el año 1951, considerada segunda madre de todos los que le siguieron. Mi madre nos cuenta que cuando Amelia tenía apenas nueve años tomó muchas de las responsabilidades en el hogar. Corría un sin número de tareas tales como cocinar y cuidar de los muchachos. Amelia era el orgullo de la familia—físicamente preciosa con una belleza natural, y más que todo una paz espiritual que todo el mundo se esmeraba por estar en su presencia. Era responsable tanto académicamente como en el hogar.

Cada año consecutivo mi madre daba a luz, llegando a un total de trece hijos, ocho hembras y cinco varones. Mi niñez fue hermosa y sana. Parte de mi adolescencia la viví detrás de la montaña. La casa era de madera y el techo de zinc. Vivíamos entre cuerdas y cuerdas de terreno. Mi padre la llamaba tierra santa porque cosechaba de todo, rodeada de montañas, ríos, árboles, vegetación, frutas y animales. Crecimos entre una magnífica belleza de árboles de china, caña de azúcar, guayaba, mangos, aguacate y flores. Crecí con la virtud de aventurar las tierras; crecí con el miedo y el respeto de lo desconocido, "las cosas de la noche."

Todo comenzó cuando apenas tenía cinco años. Era la primera vez que recuerdo que mis padres nos dejaban solos para asistir a un bautizo en el que ellos eran los padrinos. La noche en el campo era clara, el cielo lleno de estrellas y los sonidos de la noche acompañados por el canto del coquí. "Coquí, coquí, coquí, quí, quí, quí." La brisa moviendo los árboles de un lado a otro, las pequeñas piedras que con los vientos volaban y daban a caer al techo de la casa, creaban un tono de música melancólica. Nosotros sentados en el suelo de la sala con la luz encendida, mi hermana Amelia sentada en una silla tratando de entretenernos mientras nos contaba un cuento.

"Una vez y dos son tres. En las montañas vivía un matrimonio, esposo, esposa y muchos hijos. Eran tan pobres que no tenían suficiente comida. En otras palabras se estaban muriendo de hambre. Una tarde el esposo triste le dijo a su esposa, Fulana, 'La tormenta destruyó la cosecha y no hay suficiente alimento para toda la familia. Vamos a tener que votar a tres de los hijos mayores, que son los que más comen. Mujer, prepáralos que los voy a dejar detrás de la montaña. Dicen que se aparece una mamá bruja y cuida bien de los muchachos.'

"La madre con el corazón en la mano preparó a los niños. Los abrazó y les echó la bendición. El padre los tomó de la mano y los acompaño al viaje sin regreso. Comenzó un juego de escondite con los niños y al ver que los niños estaban envueltos se aprovechó de la situación y se escapó, dejando a los niños perdidos y solos. Los niños buscaron a su padre y no lo encontraron, dándose cuenta de que su padre los había abandonado. Comenzaron a llorar y a caminar hacia una cueva que vieron. Cuando entraron a la cueva una vieja mendiga les dijo. 'Bienvenidos hijitos. Llámenme mamá bruja.'" Y Amelia terminó su cuento diciendo, "Cuento acabao, que me cuenten uno más salao."

Poniendo el oído para escuchar los ruidos desconocidos, mi hermana nos decía, "Shhshs... Son cosas de la noche." Sentada en el suelo temblaba de miedo, con los ojos muy abiertos y los oídos parados tratando de distinguir los ruidos. Mientras repetíamos una oración que mi padre nos había enseñado para que Dios nos acompañara y nos elevara la fuerza espiritual:

> Dios conmigo, yo con Él,
> Él delante de mí,
> y yo atrás de Él.

La puerta de entrada era de madera bastante grande, contenía una tranca—un pedazo de madera en el medio de la puerta—que aseguraba de que nadie pudiera entrar. Carmen, la segunda, y Eduardo, el tercero en la familia y el mayor de los varones, oyeron un ruido y pensaron que eran nuestros padres. De pronto abrieron la puerta y vieron un hombre vestido de soldado en color khaki parado frente a la casa. Ellos rápidamente cerraron la puerta y comenzaron a llorar. Todos nos abrazamos y lloramos hasta que mis padres aparecieron. Les contamos nuestro dilema, jurando que todos habíamos visto al individuo. Mi madre nos alivió nuestra pena con una taza de chocolate caliente y galletitas de flores y nos recordó que no era bueno mentir porque Dios lo veía todo. Nos fuimos a dormir todos tranquilos.

Mi madre nos echó la bendición y se fue a dormir con mi padre como de costumbre. De repente, sintió un pellizcón en el brazo. Cuando miró, vió a un hombre alto vestido de soldado. El hombre le dijo, "No eran mentiras, yo cuido a tus hijos cuando tú no estás." Mi madre quedó congelada tratando de gritar y de comunicarse con mi padre pero no podía. Ella comenzó a rezarle a Dios y esto la liberó.

Desde entonces mi madre ha tenido un sin número de experiencias con este individuo llamado "Protector" de la familia Bonilla Veléz. Cuando le hacemos preguntas a mi mamá acerca de este tema, nos contesta, "Son cosas de la noche."

My mother was only fifteen years old when she married my father, who was forty-one. A year later they had their first daughter, Amelia, born in the year 1951, considered the second mother of all the children that followed. My mother tells us that when Amelia was barely nine years old, she took on a lot of the responsibilities of the house. She carried out many tasks, such as cooking and care of the children. Amelia was the pride of the family—physically lovely, with natural beauty and overall a spiritual peace which mesmerized everyone in her presence. She was as successful in school as she was at doing house chores.

Each consecutive year my mother gave birth, to a total of thirteen children, eight females and five males. My childhood was beautiful and healthy. For part of my adolescence I lived in the mountains. The house was made out of wood, with a zinc roof. We lived on acres and acres of land. My father called it a holy land because it produced a little bit of everything and was surrounded by mountains, rivers, trees, vegetation, fruits, and animals. We grew up amidst the magnificent beauty of orange bushes, sugar cane, guava, mango, avocado, and flowers. I grew up with the virtue of venturing in new lands; I grew up with fear and respect for the unknown, "the things of the night."

Everything started when I was just five years old. It was the first time I remember that my parents left us home alone, in order to attend a baptism at which they were the godparents. The night in the country was clear. The sky full of stars and the sounds of the night were accompanied by the song of the *coquí*: "*Coquí, coquí, coquí, quí, quí, quí.*" The breeze moving the trees from side to side and the small stones blowing in the wind and falling on the roof created a tone of melancholic music. We were sitting on the living room floor with the light on, my sister Amelia in a chair, trying to entertain us by telling us a story.

"Once upon a time, in the mountains there lived a couple, husband, wife, and many children. They were so poor that they did not have enough food. In short, they were dying of hunger. One afternoon the sad husband told his wife, Fulana, 'The storm destroyed the harvest and there is not enough food to feed all the family. We are going to have to get rid of the oldest three children because they are the ones that eat the most. Woman, get them ready; I am going to leave them behind the mountain, where they say there dwells a mother witch who will care for the children.'

"With her heart in her mouth, the mother prepared her children. She hugged them and gave them her blessing. The father took them by the hand and escorted them on a journey of no return. He started a hide-and-seek game with the children and, when the children were playing, took advantage of the situation and left them. He left them lost and alone. The children searched for their father and, not finding him, realized that their father had abandoned them. They started to cry and began walking toward a cave they had spotted. When they entered the cave, an old beggar woman said, 'Welcome, my children. Call me Mother Witch.'" And Amelia finished the story by saying, "Story done, and tell me a saltier one."

Listening carefully to hear the mysterious sounds, my sister kept saying, "Shhshs... those are things of the night." Sitting on the floor, I shook with fear, with my eyes wide open, listening carefully, trying to distinguish the sounds. Meanwhile we repeated a prayer my father had taught us so that God would be with us and strengthen our spiritual force:

> *God is with me and I am with Him,*
> *He is in front of me,*
> *and I am behind Him.*

The entrance door was made out of wood, with a *tranca*—a piece of wood across the door—to ensure that no one would be able to come in. Carmen, the second oldest, and Eduardo, third in the family and oldest of the boys, heard a sound and thought it was our parents. All of a sudden they opened the door and saw a man dressed as a soldier in khaki standing in front of the house. They immediately closed the door and started to cry. We all hugged each other and cried until our parents appeared. We told them about our dilemma, swearing that we all saw the man. My mother calmed our fears with a cup of hot chocolate and flower cookies, reminding us that it was not good for us to lie because God saw everything. We all went to sleep in peace.

My mother gave us her blessing and went to sleep with my father as usual. All of a sudden she felt a pinch on her arm. When she looked, she saw a tall man dressed like a soldier. The man said, "It wasn't a lie; I take care of your children when you are not around." My mother froze, trying to scream and call for my father, unable to make a sound. She started to pray to God and was released.

Since then my mother has had a series of experiences with this person called the "Protector" of the Bonilla Veléz family. When we ask her questions about this topic, she answers, "These are things of the night."

Elena Harap

POST-MODERN MOM

Six months after astronauts first walked the surface of the moon, my daughter was born. It was winter, past my due date, and at night the three bright stars of the constellation Orion assured me that everything was in sync, the baby would obey its own rhythm. Ten days we waited, until one morning she rocketed out, leaving me slightly torn but euphoric.

Jazz and popular music spoke to me of my personal condition. "Wish I could talk to you, Baby" was a mother's yearning for language in that period before her infant breaks the code and starts to talk. Thelonious Monk's "Criss Cross" was about our life in the inner city, on a one-way street three blocks long, where most people knew each other—bank clerks, dope dealers, political activists, machinists, art students, grandmothers, teachers, Buddhists, Catholics, Pentecostals, uncommitted souls, Irish, Italians, Puerto Ricans, African-Americans, Yankees, Germans, Cubans, West Indians. I could take off from this deeply layered yet familiar base to other planets. The nearby conservatory of music held a world of sounds trying to become perfect. On the next hill from ours, a mysterious, guarded commune pursued philosophy and altered mind states in a cluster of old white frame houses at the top. I criss-crossed these territories, hoping to find, or create, a place where all could meet and survive.

During my daughter's preteen years, neighborhood kids sang "Ground Control to Major Tom," which they told me was an image for tripping on drugs; I heard in it the voices of parents and adolescent children calling back and forth through space, on the journey of growing up. Nowadays the notion of "growing up" itself seems spacey and time-warped, as if I had entered that weird sequence at the end of the film "2001" where an adult character gradually returns to a fetal state. I often feel as if I have to begin all over, simply to grasp our present landscape—the AIDS epidemic, the Internet, the movement of capital across international boundaries. Youngsters sit at my computer and playfully explore its capacities while I keep repeating the same few tasks; my daughter, more aware of the future than her parents, makes me mindful of what our household uses and what we throw away. Paper napkins disappear from my kitchen in favor of cloth; I seek foods marked *organic* and pay the extra cost, in hope of a planet whose soil, water, and air are restored to health. Children represent Ground Control to me, while I am adrift, seeking a clear and responsible position.

Suspension is my daughter's natural condition. Once, when she could barely walk, I found her balancing on her stomach on a window sill as if she expected to fly right out, forty feet above the sidewalk. Another time she toddled purposefully toward the deep end of a swimming pool, ready to step in. I watched her and her team-mates—streamlined, urgent—lift off and take the hurdles at high school track meets. At the same time she was open with her feelings, vulnerable to others' hurts.

I remember how, after we had been to see "E.T.," she came out of the theatre in tears and walked into a plate glass door. She embraced the promise of space, knew the sadness of human limits.

It's twenty-five years since the nights I looked up at Orion's starred belly and felt my daughter dancing. A woman now, she chooses Vermont and the care of the land for her particular orbit. Summers when I watch her turn aerial somersaults from a high bank into the local swimming hole, she calls, "Come on and jump, Mom, it's easy." But I will not even go in feet first from that height. I trust her to land safely, though, in the cold brook water—and elsewhere.

Incantations

Aura Luz Sanchez

ENGLISH ONLY

Note: *Macana*, a policeman's nightstick.

Me no speek eengleesh, she say
to la trabajadora, l'investigadora,
americana, anglo-sajona,
republicana, suburbiana–
who come snoopin, lookin
like a human spotlight swoopin
down from a prison tower,
with a cobra neck
and clairvoyant eyes
come to catch the taboo husband
come to question the terrified migrants
come to peer down her Caucasian nose
at bargain basement Latinas
who must be taught
how to feed their children
who must be taught
how to keep their homes
who must be taught
how to know their place
who come sniffin, snoopin like a hound
with her snout liftin the sheets
snuffin out in the name of
welfare reform, welfare conform, welfare deform

Me no speek eengleesh, he say
to la policia, l'autoridad
con su revolver y su macana
who stop him, stomp him
at the lights, one night
who come searchin for his
        reg-is-tra-tion
who come searchin for drugs
cruisin, cursin, searchin
for nothin but

kicks with spics
and bashes his face
because it's brown

Me no speek eengleesh, she say
to the judge, el juez
who watches his watch
not lookin to know
why panic tears stream down her cheekbones
like rain-filled street gutters
mixed with dirt
from her man's fist on her face

Only lookin to know
when his court
will be emptied of spics
who don't even speak English

ELENA HARAP

WORDS AS
MAGICAL
INCANTATIONS

I.

Stories and magical words were among my parents' earliest gifts to me, beginning with the tale of their own romance. My parents met aboard a ship from London to New York in the summer of 1926. My father was returning from an academic conference and my mother from visiting relatives near London. As my mother tells it, "One night when nothing was doing, I decided it would be much nicer to go out and walk on the deck. And I found there was somebody else out there, walking in the opposite direction. So we walked around and passed each other at approximately the same place—nobody said anything—and finally, after four or five times, the gentleman turned around and joined up with me and he said, 'Suppose we walk together.' And that's what we did the rest of our lives." If stories like this, heard early and often, shape our perception of the world, I hold this tale—and the long and steady marriage which ensued from that first meeting—responsible for my own sometimes reckless optimism and my preference for happy endings.

My mother's delight in words was woven into her love for her family. When I was about five, she copied and bound a Christmas poem I composed. She set the lines as free verse, beginning, "A bright star shone over Bethlehem/on Christmas Eve," printing the words carefully—a departure from her normal handwriting, which was scribbly and rounded at the edges, talkative handwriting. Ordinarily the crosses on her t's flew a little above their stems, double o's had a loose, swooping line to connect them, and s's at the ends of words trailed off like the ends of wrapping ribbon on a present. I came to know this writing intimately later on when, like everyone else in the family, I became the recipient of voluminous handwritten letters from my mother. She wrote in cheerful detail about household mishaps such as lost keys or leaks in the plumbing, concerts and lectures, visitors for lunch. I did not appreciate the letters; I used to skim through them without much thought. My father, however, saved and filed the letters my mother wrote him daily during his frequent travels to schools around the country as a curriculum consultant. Manila folders packed with pages in the scrawl that hurried to keep pace with her thoughts wait now for me to read at leisure, with new respect for my mother as a historian of everyday life.

Out of my impromptu Christmas poem my mother created a neat little booklet. The verses, written on notepaper with deckle edges, were hand-stitched into a brown cardboard cover. I still think of this with surprise. There was the poem, separate from myself, transcribed and readable. It marked my first consciousness of myself as a writer. In a few years my impulse to write took independent form. On my tenth birthday someone gave me a blue bound book with a small lock and key. I began to record moments of excitement, confusion, disappointment. "May 2, 1947. This is my birthday. I got this diary. I got a puzzle from Joan, a plaster [plastic] tea set from Eileen. I'm getting *The Wind Boy* [a favorite book] and I got a satchel and $1.00. May 3. Didn't go to my birthday dinner. I cried. Mommy fixed me up. Sick today. Made my puzzle. Finished 'The Little White Horse.' Had my birthday cake tonite. Good."

Since then I have kept journals almost continuously, with much the same unabashed self-involvement. The forthright sentences written in 1947 define efforts to cope with and own my feelings and experiences, as do later experiments with dialogue, stream of consciousness, and cartoons. I copy passages from my reading and note public events. The journal is a neutral spot to which I return in times of trouble to find the voice of common sense.

In 1988 when the proofs of the first Streetfeet Women's journal, *Many Voices*, arrived in the mail, I had the same sense of revelation inspired by my mother's homemade booklet. I touched the pale blue pages and admired details of the book's design as one might marvel over the fingers and toes of a newborn baby. The package gave out a certain warmth and light, as if alive. This book was a journal of the Streetfeet company's trip to the 1985 United Nations Decade for Women Conference in Nairobi, Kenya. Red, dusty streets; women gathering by the thousands in the courtyard at the

University; the smiling, intent faces of our Kenyan hosts; moments of sudden awareness of ourselves as Americans in Africa, privileged and wealthy—regardless of our status at home—with access to education and consumer goods, watches, blue jeans, TV sets; all were gathered into this brief document. In writing and publishing the book, we completed our adventure by giving it away.

The necessity of writing is different from the choice to publish. In a daily onslaught of details and obligations, random impressions, conversations, television images, and newsprint, I affirm my sense of self by writing. As the work proceeds, patterns emerge, as scattered iron filings form designs around a magnet. Out of confusion comes peace, a poem, a new beginning.

II.

My sisters joked with me about my first poem and we made parodies of it. My older sisters taught me to read and, as far as I know, to write; perhaps they felt a sense of ownership over anything I produced. I am the third of four girls. In an era in which numbers of women come together seeking collective power, I happened to be born into a women's group. We four Harap girls had a very consistent childhood together in the same house, same school, with the same parents. My older sisters were born two-and-a-half years apart; four years later I arrived, and a year later my younger sister. We "little girls" came into a world of language that included books of poetry our mother read aloud; songs, rhymes, and jokes the "big girls" brought home from school; and our father's strong expectation that we would speak grammatical English at all times.

My parents began their married life in Ohio and moved to Nashville, Tennessee, in 1937, soon after I was born. This regional change shaped my early experience of language. I heard a spectrum of Southern accents, some soft and musical, which I associate with Virginia and the Deep South; some harder and more nasal, suggesting the mountains. While it is not true that Southerners speak slowly, Southern speech has a way of lengthening sounds that suggests relaxation and leisure, a welcoming cadence.

My world was divided into "negro" and "white." Living in a white neighborhood in Nashville, I heard little African-American speech or rural white dialect, and what I did hear was often caricature. My friends and I played a game in which, in answer to any question, we had to say, "Ol' Black Mammy's Greazy Toe" without laughing. One of our favorite comic strips, "Li'l Abner," made fun of the Appalachian Mountain dialect. Indirectly we were taught to stereotype blacks and to regard cultures other than that of the white middle class as inferior.

The South's history of slavery was embedded in our games. Rhymes I took for granted then come back with a shock now; for example, a word game that played on these lines:

> The poor old slave has gone to rest,
> I know that he is free.
> His bones they lie, disturb them not,
> 'way down in Tennessee.

My companions and I sang this in increasingly complicated forms, empty of meaning:

> The piggety-pack-poor old sliggety-slack-slave has
> giggety-gack-gone to riggety-rack-rest,
> I nigetty-nack-know that higgety-hack-he is free . . .

I made no connection between the "poor old slave" and the real-life black people whom I knew as a small child: Ludie Pearl Stott, brown-skinned, handsome and self-contained, who took care of me and my sisters; Julia Curry, a short, solid woman with burnished black skin, who came to do ironing; and a gray-brown, faded man I remember only by the name of Hopwood, an occasional gardener. As a twelve-year-old, participating in an integrated club organized by a Fisk University professor's wife, I came to know black girls my own age. While I realized that such a group was unusual for Nashville in the late 1940s, I had no sense of the society that had given rise to our separation. The ways of slavery were not examined in American history class.

My mother at ninety-one made me aware of her own childhood language of prejudice when she happened to hear the word pork in a conversation and recited, "Take a piece of pork, put it on a fork, give it to a Jew boy, Jew, Jew, Jew." This from the woman whose shipboard romance with a "Jew boy" lasted a lifetime. My daughter, hearing this, reminded me of a game she and her friends played on the front steps of our house in Boston:

> Chinese school has just begun,
> no more laughing, no more fun,
> if you show your teeth or tongue
> you will pay a penalty.

"Chinese School" in turn triggered the recollection of a children's counting song that uses Native Americans as objects, with chilling implication. "One little, two little, three little Indians," the song begins, continuing to ten, after which the numbers are reversed: "Ten little, nine little, eight little Indians," back to "one little Indian boy." Not only are Indians considered non-persons; they are made to disappear. The genocidal nineteenth-century fantasy of winning the West lives on in this banal, frightening ditty. Each culture seems to teach its own stereotypes through children's games, and there is always the unknown "other" whom the children are permitted to mock and use as they please. We begin in innocence and have to take in, then somehow transcend, the cultural lies stored in our inheritance of language.

What counter-messages did I hear, what voices defining a common humanity? My Congregational Sunday School education provides no answer, since the church and Sunday School were for whites only, the images of Jesus bland and Caucasian. I recall instead the scratchy sound of a phonograph record produced by UNESCO to convey information about the United Nations through children's songs. I played this little disk many times, to my mother's disgust. "What doggerel," she would comment to herself, aware of the reality of global war while her daughter was being entertained with platitudes about how U-N-E-S-C - O would work to make the world a better place to be -o. Yet the song I absorbed most thoroughly was a setting of the Preamble to the United Nations Charter. The cheerful voices of the chorus pounded out the text with all the subtlety of a Corn Flakes commercial; but I held on to the promise, accents and all:

> We are de-*ter*-mined
> To *make* the United Na-tions
> An *in*-strument to *put* an end to *war*.

I was aware of war as photographed by *Life* magazine correspondents; in particular, I could not erase from my mind the image of an American prisoner, hands bound, kneeling in the shadow of a Japanese soldier who held a curved sword lifted high to behead him. After listening to grownups' conversation one night, I wrote sadly in my diary, "Why do people talk about war?" War was too frightening to think about. For me, the U.N. jingle was a spell to be invoked against human violence and cruelty. "We reaffirm our faith in fundamental human rights, in equal rights for men and women," the singers chanted doggedly. Perhaps it is no coincidence that some fifty years later I find myself touring as an actress in the role of Eleanor Roosevelt, a member of the first U.N. delegation from the United States and probably the most influential person behind the framing and acceptance of the International Declaration of Human Rights.

III.

Speaking "correct" English was highly valued in our household. My father's own first language was Yiddish. He came from the province of Galicia in Eastern Europe, emigrating with his family to the Lower East Side of Manhattan in 1900, around the age of seven. Years after my father had died, I asked his younger brother, "What was the dominant language of your parents' country?" My father had never spoken a word of his experience in Europe and I was beginning to feel I had missed something important.

"Polish," said my uncle at once. "My father—your grandfather—spoke Polish and Yiddish and probably German."

"What were your Yiddish names?" I asked. His answer abruptly recast my image of my father, Henry Harap.

"Your father was Hersch, Herschl," my uncle told me. As he repeated the names, the familiar litany of relatives—Rose, Jack, Nat, Dora, Henry, Ira, Sadie, Sophie, Louis—became foreign, beckoning, available only through windows of time, custom, culture, perhaps pain and humiliation, that my father had apparently decided to keep closed. *Reisel, Yankel, Naftule, Devora, Herschl, Itzak, Sima, Leibel,* and their parents, *Yechovid* and *Moishe,* whose names I knew as Yetta and

Moses, held out a birthright both forbidding and rich with discovery. It was mine and I wanted it, all of it.

I began asking questions and studying old photographs. To begin with, I discovered that while my American surname is pronounced *Har'-up*, the old-country version, *Cha-rap'*, accents the second syllable. "The Ellis Island official who Anglicized the name must have been unusually intelligent," my uncle observed, "since he retained the form of the original, merely changing the accent and softening the guttural *ch* to an aspirate *h*."

I tried to match this new information with the persona of my father in my memory, my photo albums, in family history and hearsay. Henry Harap taught curriculum development at Peabody College for Teachers, spoke precise, deliberate English, prepared his lectures on Sunday mornings while his wife and daughters went to church and Sunday School, smoked a pipe, never did housework, played tennis with us, and took us to baseball games. *Herschl Charap* (my uncle tried patiently to get me to sound the subtle ch in the back of my mouth) spoke Yiddish, went to Hebrew School, wore high starched collars and a pince-nez, said the Kaddish, the traditional Jewish prayer for the dead, every day after his mother's death while he was a college student, and later left New York for good to build a career as a professor. In short, he became the Henry Harap who raised a family of girls to speak his adopted language according to the rules—not without humor; "*Ain't* ain't in the dictionary" was a favorite saying.

No wonder he was attracted to my mother who, besides a lively intelligence and natural sociability, possessed beautiful speech: a cultivated American accent colored by the King's English of her parents, Norah and William Chater. My mother taught elocution at Bay Ridge High School in Brooklyn. She and my father were married in Bay Ridge in 1929 and moved to Cleveland, Ohio.

Marriage anchored my father in a new culture. His Anglo-American wife, daughter of a journalist and a music teacher, came from a long line of Episcopalians. His Orthodox Jewish family ostracized the couple at first, while the Chaters, my mother's family, took to Henry warmly. Later on, my father's brothers and sisters came to know and love my mother, but at the time of the wedding some of them sat *shiva*, a ritual of mourning, for my father. His marriage was regarded as a death. As far as I know, my mother never met her father-in-law.

I could never persuade my father to reminisce about the

past, Europe, or his family. As a child I accepted this reticence, since he was generally a quiet man, and I did not feel deprived. All the same, a dense silence surrounded his childhood experience. Later I speculated—did my grandparents get out of Europe to avoid a pogrom? To keep my father from being conscripted into the Polish or the Austrian army? Did the family lie about his age and keep this a secret? Did he reject the Yiddish language so fiercely that he literally could not remember events that belonged to the Yiddish-speaking period of his life? From my father's point of view, silence may have provided safety. It gave us, his daughters, an unencumbered American birthright and a certain freedom to define ourselves, as women, with none of the restrictions of an Orthodox upbringing. But it also removed half of our inheritance. Having dealt with the loss of his mother long before he was married, my father perhaps never imagined that we children needed our grandmother, if only to know her in stories. Not even a photograph of her was in our house. He did not say whether his thoughts of his mother and father were painful or happy.

The result was that I grew up in the decidedly monolingual culture of my Chater forebears. My mother used to read us the poems of Robert Louis Stevenson, A. A. Milne, and Eleanor Farjeon, from anthologies for children. *One Hundred Best Poems for Boys and Girls*, with its familiar blue and white cover, was cheaply made in the Depression; now its pages shred and crack at the corners, falling loose from their thin binding. But the delicate black silhouettes at the head of each poem evoke the words as magical incantations. *Zoon, zoon, cuddle and croon*, began a lullaby full of images of silver light, fishes, oceans, stars. The ocean, which I had never seen, held a sense of adventure, fed by other poems: "The Pirate Don Dirk of Dowdee" and "The Owl and the Pussycat"—whose characters ended up in "the land where the Bong-tree grows," dancing on the sand by moonlight. The language of my favorite poems was musical and sensual.

> Slowly, silently, now the moon
> Walks the night in her silver shoon...

began Walter de la Mare's "Silver." I copied the mysterious lines into a notebook of my own.

Certain word patterns remain hopelessly embedded in my brain. Trivial or profound, they surface unexpectedly when I am taking a walk, writing in my journal, or having a conversation. Sentimental hymns from Sunday School emerge intact; so do

Shakespearean sonnets. When I have to memorize a theatre script, this habit of storing words is very useful. But the purpose of my childhood brain in retaining certain texts is not clear to me. Maybe all those poems about the moon helped me to accept the darkness of night and gave me through their sounds and rhythms the possibility of trusting the universe enough to relax and go to sleep. Although I don't remember having many nightmares, I do recall lying awake while my mother sleepily settled into bed with me, telling me to clear my mind. My mind was a great clutter.

My father introduced me to the fastidious demands of editing and revision. He pursued a lifelong concern for consumer education and published a series of pamphlets on topics such as "A Consumer Looks at Discount Houses" and "Politics and the Consumer." When the galleys arrived, my father would ask me to proofread with him. I felt important and useful, reading aloud from the long pages of type while he checked them against his manuscript. Red-inked notes and symbols accumulated in the margins as we worked through the text, adding, deleting, correcting.

I planned to become a teacher, not a writer, although I loved books and made my own, copying favorite poems and pasting in illustrations cut from publishers' catalogues my father brought home. Teaching was a natural choice of profession; both parents had followed it, and our family felt secure in the academic community of Peabody College, where my father worked. There was fulfillment and dignity in my father's daily routine of putting on a freshly ironed shirt and neat suit—dark blue or gray in winter, white in summer, arming himself with a briefcase of notes, and setting off early to his orderly office with green plants in the windows, where the secretary addressed him as Dr. Harap. Over the years he tried to teach a succession of secretaries to say "Mr." "*Doctor* is for M.D.'s," my father insisted. But the Southern preference for titles prevailed.

I occasionally sat in on my father's class, in a dusty lecture room with shallow semicircular tiers of seats. He did not covet the spot in the center but organized classes to run themselves. Once he visited my own classroom at Northeastern University in Boston, when I was starting out, with my newly earned Master's degree, to teach English composition. The room was an engineers' drafting studio. The students, all men, were scattered about on stools at high desks, while I led the discussion from my post at the blackboard in front. My father took one look and said, "Why don't we move our seats?" In minutes he had reassembled the group in a circle at the back of the room, a democratic and sociable configuration.

My mother did not continue teaching elocution after her marriage, though she went on to graduate school and wrote a master's thesis on the eighteenth-century diarist Samuel Pepys. After that, her life was committed to the raising of daughters, the support of her husband's career, and always the writing of letters. The advent of drip-dry, no-iron shirts must have been a great relief to my mother after having provided crisp shirts to go with Henry's neatly pressed suits every morning, year after year. She took seriously the task of guiding four young women as we learned to walk and talk, read and write, swim, cook, choose clothes, drive a car, hold a job, entertain friends, go on dates, cope with disappointments, and find footing in the adult world. With regard to careers she was a realist, as was my father. In the field of education one could earn a living. They never told me not to become a writer or a musician; they did assume that I would be able to support myself. I took the path of least resistance. Two of my sisters also became teachers. Whether these choices were driven by being female I am not sure, since there

were no brothers with whom to compare ourselves.

I am still working with the legacies of my father and mother, discovering them in my body and personality: blue eyes from the Chaters, straight and pointed nose from the Haraps, inability to remember geographical directions from the Haraps, stiff-upper-lip self-control from the Chaters. My left-handedness—I don't know where that comes from; no one in my immediate family has it. From my mother, a big behind and flyaway hair. From my father, the way my neck and lower face thicken with age.

For years I believed in the mystique of inspiration. The power to write announced itself unequivocally, I assumed, and the person so gifted knew instinctively that writing was her life work. In my early teens I met a high school senior who planned to become a novelist, admired him from a distance, and read Huxley's *Eyeless in Gaza* just so that I could discuss it with him. We were members of a discussion group for "gifted children," and in a session about writing I commented, "I write a lot of letters." The adults in the room were amused and I felt foolish. It took the women's movement of the 1970s and later the Streetfeet Women to bring the conviction that writing a lot of letters might lead to something more ambitious—essays, a play, a novel. Accepting the myth of the genius author allowed me to avoid for a long time a commitment to the persistent, everyday work of serious writing.

IV.

Music was the force that made me confront my writing self. I was raised on Western classical music, played flute in the Nashville Youth Orchestra during high school, and had a job as an extra in the Nashville Symphony. Music-making was vital, immediate, an approach to sexuality—the giddy complexity of a symphony orchestra in rehearsal, intensity of sight-reading Baroque chamber music in an ensemble group, intimacy of the cell-like soundproof listening rooms where I would go to hear classical records or jazz with one of the boys in our circle of school musicians. At the Symphony I remember Debussy's "Nuages" and "Sirènes" for orchestra and women's chorus. The woodwind section where I sat was in the middle of the orchestra, in a seascape of sound, and the chromatic patterns of the music touched me seductively. At school there were day trips to state music festivals in other towns—something enticing and romantic about being among new people, meeting boys during rehearsals, judging sessions and lunch breaks, the crowded bus with its early morning departures and nighttime returns.

Inside our school building an ambience of privileged initiation pervaded the Vault, a basement storage room for musical instruments, with its heavy, black-painted steel door into which was set an imposing combination lock the size of a saucer. Battered brass bells of tubas and sousaphones propped themselves against the walls of the Vault. Trombones, trumpets and flutes in need of repair lay about in their worn cases. We musicians would drop in to borrow instruments or talk shop, the savvy jazz improvisers who played by ear impressing docile classical types, like myself, who depended upon a score.

The music world, like that of my childhood games, was saturated with racism. In 1954 a young Nashville Youth Orchestra conductor proposed that the group desegregate. Every musical activity I knew was segregated—the Symphony, school music festivals, church choirs. The conductor's radical proposal was voted in by the Youth Orchestra players, and colorblind auditions were held.

After five black students had been accepted, some taking first chair in their sections, and had attended a rehearsal, the trustees of the orchestra informed the group that they would not countenance these students' membership. Major donors to the Nashville Symphony, the Youth Orchestra's parent group, threatened to withdraw their support. There were meetings, letters; the young conductor resigned his post; a black student flutist, Lois Wheeler, and I were invited to New York to be part of a New York *Herald Tribune* Forum on desegregation. We sat on the stage in the Hunter College auditorium and played a Telemann duet; we met Thurgood Marshall. Yet nothing really happened. The orchestra went back to being segregated, and the trustees hired a new conductor. I remember thinking that we had to accept the adults' decision, otherwise there would be no orchestra at all. I did not comprehend true change or see myself as an agent of change. But the experience left an undercurrent of turmoil: I had taken part in a clearly immoral action. By accepting the status quo, I had allowed myself to become a poorer, meaner person.

My high school is no longer segregated. Nashville Symphony applicants now audition behind a screen. The flutist with whom I went to the Forum in New York went on to become a professional musician and the first chair player in another Southern city's symphony orchestra. Nothing since then has tested me in the way that the Youth Orchestra experience did. In the context of Streetfeet I look at that girl growing up "white" in Tennessee; I listen to Mary McCullough's accounts of growing up "colored" in Virginia and begin to examine with new awareness the fabric of ignorance that insulated me in the Fifties. Slowly I begin to hear the stories that existed around me, another rhythm, another music.

As a college student majoring in English, I gradually gave up flute lessons and regular practice. After college came years of teaching, graduate school and my marriage in 1964. My future husband's enthusiasm for classical music endeared him to me. In the glove compartment of his green Volkswagen bug he carried a sheaf of operatic arias copied onto sheets of music paper. When he had a free moment, he would take out this music and sing it for fun.

We settled in Boston's Mission Hill neighborhood, where my husband started a woodworking shop, and here we began raising our son and daughter. I came to define myself as a House Musician, a player in private settings—home, community center, church. The link that existed for me between music and sexuality remains. I associate the sheer heady joy of entering into the musical conversation of the woodwind quintet—flute, oboe, clarinet, bassoon, French horn—with lovemaking, a joy that also overtakes me sometimes when I am writing.

I did not write during the late Sixties and early Seventies. It was a time of turbulent experience—becoming a parent, beginning theatre study, getting to know a multi-ethnic urban neighborhood, balancing part-time work in a Roxbury settlement house with family responsibilities, witnessing the school busing crisis in Boston, confronting world events and the impact of the Civil Rights movement. College students went door-to-door on our street, protesting the Vietnam War and U.S. intervention in Cambodia; women friends started a consciousness-raising group; hippies and runaways congregated on the Boston Common. The more complex the outer texture of life, the more I began to need an inner space in which to reflect on my world.

As my children grew older, I wanted to get back to flute-playing. The rhythm of the city had gotten into my bones, making me search for sounds that could adequately interpret my experience. I joined a jazz improvisation workshop at the New England Conservatory, where in drab little basement cubicles I practiced augmented fourths in sequence, ascending and descending major sevenths. Every so often I would put the flute aside and jot down descriptions of people: the other players in my jazz ensemble, mothers I met at my children's school, neighbors on the street. I hardly admitted to myself that I was drafting poems, but the sketches kept coming. I began to work on them outside of the practice room, then talked with a poet friend, Kathleen Spivack, about what I was doing. "Put your poems in groups," she advised, and a collection, "Portraits of Sisters," took shape. In 1980 it became the Streetfeet Women's first performance piece. I never learned to "play on the changes," but I can thank my encounter with jazz at the Conservatory for the solitude in which I could start to write.

V.

Although poems continued to surface, theatre became my focus during the Seventies and Eighties. On the street, in sandy playgrounds, on the small wood-paneled stage at the public library or the larger stage of the local elementary school auditorium, I produced neighborhood plays with my children, their friends, my husband and other parents, and a circle of professional dancers, actors, designers, musicians. Our plays reflected the city as we knew it. "The Wizard of Oz" became "El Mago de Oz," with Dorothy transformed to Dorotea, a rural Puerto Rican child making her way in the Emerald City of Boston. Menotti's opera and miracle play "Amahl and the Night Visitors" unfolded against a backdrop on which the artist painted Boston triple-decker houses and the towers of the Mission Church, a neighborhood landmark where faith healings were known to have taken place: crutches festooned the chapel beside the main altar to confirm it.

In trying to solve problems of a production, I would concentrate on a space, filled with images, which seemed to hover in my upper body, inside my rib cage. Sometimes the space was an utterly plain room with a wooden table and one candle burning on it; other times it contained voices giving advice—no-nonsense pronouncements by three raucous, impudent crows from the movie "The Wiz," for example. Now in Vermont in the Nineties I don't seem to have access to the same colorful, three-dimensional inner place. Perhaps it is unnecessary. I have my own studio adorned with rugs, paintings, calligraphy, masks, family pictures—a stage set of my life. Outside the window is a different kind of drama. Shadblow blooms white in spring, a celebration; winter snowstorms, very silent, envelop the house and slow down the rhythm of a day.

In the country I am drawn to observe small events. In spring each unassuming bud on the mountain ash tree unfolds layer upon layer of elegant, pointed leaves, lined up precisely in pairs along a thin stem, each leaf a cool gray-green with delicate saw-toothed edges. All over the tree they open and open, like books or like hands, emerging flawless from their brown sheaths, until the bare twigs disappear and the tree stands in a cloud of silvery green. The realization that this magnificence is commonplace—it happens, in one form or another, on every tree—is overwhelming. Where the city called me to fashion music and theatre to play out human stories, the country makes me a spectator. A pond needs no director, no designer. It is endlessly in motion and full of cross-rhythms. The flight of insects just above the surface plays against the darting of polliwogs in shadows of floating dead leaves; frogs leap to safety at my footstep, then plant themselves in shallow water like impassive sentries and occasionally, with deadly swiftness, catch a fly.

In Vermont I return to a time when at eight or nine I explored our Nashville neighborhood at will. There was a creek to follow, bordering large, grassy back yards where one family kept chickens and another had the best swing set in the neighborhood. In the humid summer, streets were lazy and I was busy being part of that laziness. Squatting by a pond in Vermont to watch frogs on a June day, I reenter the timeless state I enjoyed in summer seasons as a child.

VI.

The Streetfeet Women, coming together to write and perform in 1982, brought me back to family legacies. When we were composing a theatre piece to take to the 1985 U.N. Women's Conference in Nairobi, Kenya, the Company challenged me to interrupt my father's silence. We were planning a sequence on grandmothers, reflecting the ways women of our families had been controlled and oppressed. Mary spoke of the rapes of black slave women in the South, Li Min of Chinese women's bound feet, and Blanca of the burden of illiteracy for Puerto Rican women. I had heard that at the time of her marriage, my grandmother Yetta was required by Orthodox Jewish custom to cut off her hair and wear a wig—the *scheytl*. The aunt who told me said she had never seen her mother's hair; women's beautiful hair was thought to be too seductive, unseemly, once they were married. We used this in our piece, "Many Voices," and decided to add lullabies in the various languages of the grandmothers, as well as a litany of lines in English, Chinese, Spanish, and Yiddish. I was stuck. Yetta had died long before I was born; no one ever sang or talked to me in Yiddish. Encouraged by my colleagues, I learned a tender Hebrew lullaby from a Theodore Bikel song book. I wrote to the Yiddish Book Clearing House in Holyoke, Massachusetts for a translation of our closing piece, then appealed to the wife of one of my Harap cousins for help with pronunciation. Eventually I could deliver my lines: *Dos zen durkh andere oygn, dos hern mit andere oyern*, seeing [life] through different eyes, hearing it with different ears.

I did not pursue an acquaintance with Grandmother Yetta, but she came back anyway. Sitting in my sister's garage in Maryland one May weekend in 1986, I went through boxes and files saved after my father's death five years before. Among letters, check stubs, graduation programs, and family wedding announcements was a worn black notebook, tall and narrow, like a small ledger, bound in soft leather, closely written. The first entry was Dec. 31, 1911. This was my father's journal, and as I leafed through it I found statements of naked grief at the death of his mother in 1913. "A hopeless wreck has befallen me but out of the wreck there arises the hope of doing better and nobler things, of helping the oppressed, of kindness and truth. We all await the return of our mother [from the hospital] but no longer alive. My mother is dead! My mother is gone! She never will return . . . . The body arrives, & is washed. I hardly thought I was alive. We all follow the hearse . . . . Our solemn shiva service continues. Daven [pray] in morning & say 'Kaddish,' have breakfast but not cooked by my mother . . . sit last day of shiva . . . Put my shoes on for 1st time in week. To synagogue & Kaddish. Home for supper." I wept for my father's loss and for my own.

Sadness, curiosity and a determination to reclaim what was lost brought me some years later to a workshop with the poet Martín Espada, in the company of Streetfeet members Aura Sanchez and Li Min Mo. Aura had been working with family history to create a set of poems, "Love Story," each in a different voice. I wanted to try the same approach and, to my surprise, some of the Harap women began to "speak" to me, first an aunt and then my grandmother herself. I struggled to hear them and put down what they said. In the workshop I shaped these statements into fictional monologues, and felt more fully my relationship to these kinswomen.

Streetfeet seems part of a pattern of women's gatherings that teach and nurture, in the fabric of my life, beginning with my female circle of siblings. A conversation with an older sister, however, warned me how close memory is to fiction. I asked, "Do you remember teaching me to read?" She replied unsentimentally, "I think you probably taught yourself." The image of solicitous big sisters reading aloud and coaching me abruptly dropped away and an annoying pest appeared, crouching in corners over storybooks and ambushing the "big girls" to get them to explain a hard word or show her what book they were reading. Both pictures, no doubt, are correct. Whatever the process, I still believe in the nurturing, I am still attempting ambush, and language is still the prize.

BLANCA BONILLA

TRADICIONES BONILLA/BONILLA TRADITIONS

Cuando vivíamos en Puerto Rico, mi padre tenía su propio plato de un tamaño grandísimo; y de costumbre cenábamos juntos todos los días. La cena con la familia era sagrada. Mi padre y madre se sentaban en sillas y nosotros nos sentabamos en el suelo alrededor de ellos. Cuando terminábamos con nuestra cena hacíamos una fila para recibir la cuchara de la bendición. Mi padre nos daba a todos una cuchara llena de su comida. Uno por uno le pedíamos la bendición y mi padre con tan buena voluntad nos echaba la bendición todos los días. Era el regalo especial del día.

El rosario se rezaba todos los días, era parte de nuestras vidas. Era sagrado unirnos como una familia antes de acostarnos y darle las gracias al Señor por todas sus bendiciones del día. Como cenábamos así nos colocábamos para rezar el rosario que duraba unos treinta minutos. Aunque nos quejábamos de vez en cuando, mis padres nos recordaban de la necesidad de evaluar y apreciar la vida que teníamos. Una de las hermanas mayores leía las letanías.

> Santa María
> Ruega por nosotros (Respondíamos)
> Santa madre de Dios
> Ruega por nosotros (Respondíamos)
> Santa Virgen de las vírgenes
> Ruega por nosotros (Respondíamos)
> Santa de la divina gracia
> Ruega por nosotros (Respondíamos)
> Madre de Jesucristo
> Ruega por nosotros (Respondíamos)
> Madre del Salvador
> Ruega por nosotros (Respondíamos)

Al mudarnos a Boston, poco a poco se fueron perdiendo esas costumbres de familia por un sin número de razones—independencia, cambios con horarios de trabajo y la escuela. Las prioridades para los hijos ya habían cambiado por las responsabilidades de vivir en una grande ciudad. La cena se hizo imposible coordinar.

Mi madre cocinaba todos las días pero no comíamos al mismo tiempo. Aunque continuamos con el rosario por más de diez años, rezándolo solamente los miércoles y los sábados; estábamos tratando de aprovechar las oportunidades de desarrollo económico sin darnos cuenta que nos alejábamos de la tradición Bonilla que mi padre sembró y cultivó hasta que nos despedimos de nuestro hogar, dulce hogar.

When we lived in Puerto Rico, my father had his own huge plate and we always had dinner together every day. The family dinner was sacred. My father and mother would sit in chairs and we sat around them on the floor. When we finished dinner, we usually made a line to receive the blessing spoon. My father gave each of us a spoonful of his food. One by one we asked for a blessing, and my father, with his good will, gave us his blessing every day. It was a special daily gift.

The rosary was said each day; it was part of our lives. It was sacred to gather as a family before going to bed and to give thanks to God for his daily blessings. Just as we ate, we used to say the rosary, which lasted thirty minutes. Although we complained sometimes, my parents reminded us of the necessity to evaluate and appreciate our life. One of my older sisters read the litany.

> Holy Mary
> Pray for us (We responded)
> Holy Mother of God
> Pray for us (We responded)
> Holy Virgin of virgins
> Pray for us (We responded)
> Holy of the divine grace
> Pray for us (We responded)
> Mother of Jesus Christ
> Pray for us (We responded)
> Mother of the Savior
> Pray for us (We responded)

When we moved to Boston, little by little we started to lose those family traditions, for a number of reasons—independence, changes in work hours, and school. The priorities for the children had changed, due to the responsibilities of living in a big city.

Dinner was impossible to coordinate with everyone and although my mother cooked every day, we did not get to eat at the same time. However, we continued with the rosary for more than ten years, saying it only on Wednesdays and Saturdays. We were trying to take advantage of opportunities for economic development, without realizing that we were moving away from the Bonilla tradition my father planted and cultivated until we finally said goodbye to our home, sweet home.

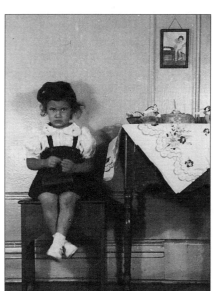

AURA LUZ SANCHEZ

DOUBLE DUTCH ON EAST 152ND STREET

As in the country-side when the days start get-ting warmer and you hear the awakening chorale of spring, so it was in the 1940s and '50s in the South Bronx on East 152nd Street, the street where I grew up. The ice man, like the sparrows, saw us through the winter. I-i-ce, i-i-ce, i-i-ce, he would bellow as the tenants descended flights of stairs to purchase their blocks of ice. As the warm days increased, so did the number of vendors. Some came with push-carts, others with horse-drawn wagons, each calling out their wares.

Vendors were not the only singers. Kids could not resist the temptation of hanging on to the backs of carts to get a free ride, and onlookers could not resist snitching on these kids. It seemed everyone knew the tune and in round-like fashion would shout, Ki-i-ds behi-i-nd, ki-i-ds behi-i-nd. Mothers had their own mantras for beckoning children to the dinner table. As evening's cloak was gently lain on the shoulders of the neighborhood, each mom opened her window to call her child indoors: Papo, Papo, Titi, Titi, Socorro-o-o.

In the summer the block was transformed from a black-and-white movie set with a scattering of performers to a technicol-or musical with a multitude of walk-ons—bearded, religious Jews, scruffy Puerto Rican children, nuns in black and white habits walk-ing two by two, ruddy-faced Irish cops on foot beats. That the block was crowded with apartment buildings, bodegas, and local variety stores—Jack's dry goods, Sal, the Italian cobbler, and the local cor-ner pharmacy, where you could go if you got something in your eye and have the pharmacist remove it with a Q-tip for free—added to a setting of sheer vibrancy. Our building was flanked on either side by storefronts. One was owned by Don Ramón, who sold nickel candy and *mavi*, a Puerto Rican drink made from the bark of a Caribbean tree. A seedy-looking man once offered to buy me an ice cream cone to replace the one I had just bought at Don Ramón's and dropped all over his wooden floor. Barely thanking the man, I took it hurriedly and ran upstairs, remembering my mother's warnings about strangers. Ironically, his kind gesture became a reason for fearing him whenever he was around.

The other storefront was usually occupied by Gypsies. We rarely had anything to do with the Gypsies, whose nomadic existence did not warrant the trouble of befriending them, but one summer when I was about seven or eight Ruby, a Gypsy girl my age, moved in with her family. Ruby was a free spirit who happily acquiesced to the stereotype of the Gypsy as fortune teller. Fortunes were told in the stairwell under the first floor landing in the building next to ours. My sister and I filled Ruby in on the neighborhood gossip, mostly about who had a crush on whom. We then raved to our friends about Ruby's clairvoyant powers, adding that for a nickel she would tell their fortunes. Ruby, no fool, allowed us to perpetrate this scam only if she derived the greater portion of the proceeds.

After my mother warmed to the idea that Ruby had become my friend, she decided to make her more acceptable. First she gave her one of my dresses, a light yellow piqué with puffy sleeves. Ruby loved the dress. My mother washed her hair and put it up in *moños*, curlers made out of strips of brown paper bag, which rendered her head a lovely bunch of chestnut banana curls. The new dress and curled hair stole much of Ruby's mystique and charm; I wished my mother had left her alone. It didn't matter, however. As soon as her own mom saw how ridiculous she looked, Ruby had to get back into her satiny, ankle-length wine-colored skirt and midriff top. The next day her hair was exotically limp again. My mother was offended, after all the work she had put into my friend's makeover. Ruby's family did not stay long—like all the other Gypsies, they left in less than a year.

For me and my cousins, the hot summer days were filled with street games, outings and running errands. A favorite of mine was *Doña Ana no esta aquí*, Doña Ana is not here, a circle game with Doña Ana in the middle. The encirclers would ask Doña Ana how she was feeling, *Como estas, Doña Ana?* Every time she was asked, she responded with a different ailment—*un dolor de cabeza*, a headache; *un dolor en la rodilla*, a knee ache; and so on—until she finally informed us, in the eeriest, most quivery voice the player could muster, that she was *m-u-e-r-t-a*, dead. We ran away, shrieking wildly, to escape from this walking dead crone, who chased us relentlessly until she caught the next Doña Ana and the game started over again. Roller skating, jumping rope, and playing ball were other daily pastimes. I never mastered Double Dutch, a high-skill jump rope game that required jumping two ropes at once as they moved in opposite directions, but I was good at the jump rope contests. You had to jump in as soon as your predecessor jumped out. The hardest was Contest One: you jumped in for one jump and jumped out while the next girl had to follow up without skipping a beat. If you failed you were "out" and became an "ender," a rope turner. If a girl was not up to jumping, she could volunteer to be a "steady ender," freeing up more time for jumpers to jump.

Although the war had been over for several years, military themes still invaded our jump rope rhymes. One went like this:

> *Officer, Officer, do your duty,*
> *here comes [the jumper], the American beauty.*
> *She can wiggle, she can waggle,*
> *she can do what she will,*
> *but she can't pull up her dress*
> *above her knees like* THIS!

At which point you were supposed to pull your skirt up above your knees with both hands, make sure you kept your balance, and exit the large arc of air and clothesline rope that framed the game. Another rhyme was:

> *Sailor, Sailor, dressed in blue,*
> *these are the orders that I must do:*
> *salute to the Captain, bow to the Queen,*
> *turn your back to the submarine.*

And in that order you saluted, bowed, and turned while jumping. Jump rope was a girls' game. The goal was not to trip on a jump and be "out." Boys' only venture into the sport was to jump in uninvited, and mischievously attempt to foul up a girl's perfect jump. Jumping rope, like roller-skating, was imbued with a sense of defiance of gravity and of the everyday, even if the levity and triumph lasted only split seconds. Like frogs leaping, we exhilarated in the rainbow of circumscribed air that suspended us. These pastimes were our first conscious experience of mastering a skill, and we welcomed them with passion and excitement as we tumbled down the stairs to greet each summer day and begin the serious act of playing.

If we got tired of jump rope, we played ball, always with a Spaldeen we bought for fifteen cents. Spaldeens were the color of unchewed chewing gum, about the size of a tennis ball, and had a lot of bounce when they were new. They were used for stickball, handball, and bouncing ball games. One game required that the ball hit a popsicle stick placed on the ground equidistant from the two players, and be caught on the bounce by the other player. Another was based on the alphabet: "A, my name is Aura and my husband's name is Al, we come from Alabama and we sell Apples; B, my name is Barbara and my husband's name is Burt, we come from Bermuda and we sell Bananas," and so on. After each alphabetical word, you crossed your leg over the bouncing ball. Bouncing and thinking on your feet were not as easy as might appear. The winner successfully got through the alphabet without missing a letter on a bounce.

On sweltering days the key to keeping cool came in the shape of a monkey wrench. A couple of twists and turns and the cold gushing waters from the fire hydrant came forth to cool off the block. Although the use of this water for such seemingly frivolous reasons did create a shortage in the homes, the women seemed not to mind, usually compensating by filling huge pots of water to ensure a supply throughout the day. This was before the days of sprinklers and neighborhood pools, before there was any consciousness that poor kids in crowded city blocks might enjoy some ways of cooling down.

Older kids would ingeniously place wooden crates over the mouths of the hydrants, creating high, vigorous showers. Teenage boys ran after the teenage girls, especially if the girls were all dressed up, and forced them into the gushing water. Although the girls would scream and yell and carry on, I think it was all feigned flirtation—pre-courtship and mating dances under the homemade waterfalls of our treeless forest.

Our waterfalls did not last long; there was always some sour soul who called the police. Minutes before the fun-killers arrived, a chorus chanted "La Hara, La Hara, La Hara." (Years later, in a sociology class, I would read that La Hara was a distortion of the name O'Hara, a tough Irish cop from the early Forties.) Amidst this melodious warning, a scurry of lawbreakers ensued as they looked to hide the evidence, the monkey wrench. Once it was even hidden under my sister's doll carriage mattress. All went back to normal until the heat once more proved unbearable, and the brave and brazen boys of East 152nd Street sallied forth with the irrepressible monkey wrench.

Games in the summer were often interrupted by errands. One of mine was to play *la bolita*—to play the numbers—for my mother. She played only when she received a premonition about a particular number. Usually this mystical insight came in dreams. If she dreamt that my Aunt Paquíta was coming from Mayaguez with her eight children on the seventh of July, she might interpret this as a sign that she should play some combination of 877. Such a message was not to be ignored, and off to the *bolitero's*, the bookie's house, I was sent.

The *bolitero* and his wife, Doña Elena, lived on the third floor of one of the buildings on my block. They were reported to have more *cucarachas* than anyone else on their street. Alas, they were under a lot of pressure from their neighbors not to spray the place with pesticide because, the neighbors were convinced, the only thing spraying did was to send the roaches off to everyone else's apartments. The situation was made worse by the dumbwaiter used to move garbage cans from the apartments to the basement, where the super collected and put them out on garbage day, allowing easy roach invasion among the apartments. The *cucarachas* were driving the couple crazy, and every day they waited to hear if they'd been accepted as tenants into the projects, where their names had been added to the long list of those desperate for this government-run panacea.

Elena was better able to control the people than the domesticated insects entering her home. She unlatched a series of locks, including a police lock, but kept the chain on, allowing the door to open about six inches. "*Quién es?*" she asked as she fidgeted forever with the multitude of locks. I responded, scared and barely audible, "*La hija de Elisa*," Elisa's daughter. With an annoyed look at having to strain to this child's voice, Elena showed the middle third of her face. I handed her the money and a strip of brown bag—a multi-purpose item in our home—where my mother had written the delphic numbers after a long search had turned up a Number Two pencil under the sofa. Down the stairs I ran, feeling much the same as after going to Confession. A hard task had been accomplished, and instead of the possibility of dying and going to heaven there was the possibility of hitting the numbers and going to heaven-on-earth, Puerto Rico! I'd never been there but had constructed an idyllic view of the island and imagined my mother as a little girl, walking with her sisters, wearing beautiful white, full-skirted eyelet dresses. So the daydream went, all the way down three flights of stairs.

It was with sadness and anticipation of things to come that I greeted the waning days of summer. By late August I felt as if I had eaten too many sweets and someone more disciplined than I would have to remove the bowl. September was exciting—back-to-school clothes, the early morning crispness that energized my mind and body, preparing them for long Catechism and penmanship lessons, and my birthday month, with recognition coming not only from my street playmates but from school friends as well.

Ethnology in those early years was simple. First there were the Puerto Ricans, divided into whites and *trigenos*-—dark-skinned— and further, into those with "good hair" and "bad hair," bad hair being extremely curly or kinky. All these subdivisions could be either Catholic or Pentecostal: you could be white, kinky-haired, and Pentecostal; dark, straight-haired, and Catholic; or any other permutation. The rest of the world was divided into the Jews, Italians, and Irish. I knew a lot more about the Irish than about any other group in our neighborhood because I attended St. Anselm's Catholic School on Tinton Avenue, where there was a heavily Irish-American congregation and student body. My sister and I were among the very few Puerto Ricans in the school. St. Anselm's was a school, church, rectory and convent, all occupying a block that was to serve as a moral epicenter for me, surrounded by an aura of sanctity that was impermeable to the poverty and drugs, the vibrancy and passion, that abutted it. Puerto Ricans, for the most part, attended public school. Perhaps this was because tuition at St. Anselm's was one dollar a month plus the cost of uniforms and books; perhaps it was because Irish Catholicism was too strict and too sterile for Puerto Ricans, devoid of Afro-Indian traditions, not allowing reinforcement of prayer with spiritualistic communication. Seeking the healing of a *curandero* bordered on the sacrilegious in the Catholicism of the Irish.

In school I admired a girl with golden curls, Barbara James, and was in love with the handsomest, smartest boy in the class, a boy with deep blue eyes, Joseph McGovern. The Jameses symbolized the values which we all knew our families could never attain.

Barbara had pale, freckled skin, lovely long banana curls and took ballet lessons. Her father, a doctor, was the only professional in the neighborhood. The family's home and practice were right next to St. Anselm's, within the protective penumbra of the Holy Roman Catholic Church. Barbara and her sister Maureen were always chosen to do solo ballets, three times a year, when students put on plays for the parents. In all my years at St. Anselm's I don't think I spoke to either Barbara or Joseph more than once or twice, but in my daydreams and fantasies they were ever-present.

There was much excitement around the time of school plays, especially on St. Patrick's Day. There was an evening of jigs and reels, and I learned quickly how to do many complex leg kicks; nonetheless, the dance teacher, Mrs. Stapleton, always relegated me to the third or fourth row to kick behind a more authentic-looking colleen. St. Anselm's also had a drum-and-bugle corps and majorettes, who marched in the parade on Fifth Avenue in Manhattan—boys with freckles blowing bugles, beating drums; girls with turned-up noses and bouncing banana curls twirling batons; and me, the girl with the unheard-of name and the *café con leche* complexion.

Many years later, back in New York visiting my family on March 17, I turned on the television out of nostalgia, to watch the St. Patrick's Day parade. St. Anselm's was still marching the drum-and-bugle corps, with the same uniforms and the same shamrock insignia, still playing "The Minstrel Boy." Although I was surprised to see them, what really shocked me was that there were black and brown hands beating the drums, holding the colors and twirling the batons, black and brown lips blowing into the fifes. The face of the neighborhood had changed over the decade, yet while tenements were razed and housing projects were replacing them, the neo-romanesque Holy Roman Catholic Church on Tinton Avenue in the South Bronx was still there.

I was a quiet child in school, always afraid that the nuns were going to slap me for walking down the aisle the wrong way or not giving the right answer. I was usually one of the smartest kids in the class, repeatedly surprising my teachers, who tended to think of Puerto Ricans as dumb. Once, in fifth grade, Sister Mary Asunta pointed me out to another nun, saying, to my confusion and hurt, "This one is very different—she's a nice girl and she's bright." The nuns' antipathy to my being Puerto Rican was greatly responsible for implanting deep ambivalences about myself, my ethnicity, and above all, my religion. How could God, if he were all-knowing and all-merciful, entrust with his faith these creatures dressed in such ugly habits, these fearsome women who made me feel so wrong and worthless even as I was getting straight A's and adoring St. Lucy, St. Teresa, and the Blessed Virgin Mary.

Home and school were two different worlds for me, like the rope game of Double Dutch, each rope independent of the other, turning with equal force in opposite directions. In addition to the impossible demands of the Dominican nuns of St. Anselm's, at home I had to deal with a pretty, awful-tempered older sister. Virginia was five years older than I and made it very clear that she detested me. When I was a baby, she got even with me for being born by cleaning her chalkboard erasers on my infantile eczema. Still, I adored her, kept all her secrets, and—like the Catholic martyrs in our Religion class reader—often took the rap for her if that would bring me into her good graces.

While I was the child who hid between my mother's legs and behind her skirts when confronted with new people, Virginia demanded center stage. My sister loved to perform; it was only my total dedication to her that allowed me to conquer my shyness and play a supporting role in the scenarios she produced and directed. My cousins and I were assigned minor parts, while Virginia was the star, and rightfully so. Hadn't she thought it up? Weren't the beautiful crepe paper costumes her idea? Wasn't she the only one gutsy enough to require a roomful of adults, drinking and dancing and having a great time, to sit quietly and put up with our precociousness?

Virginia did not limit her audience to indulgent relatives. She counted the faculty and students of St. Anselm's as members of her fan club and was even able to get the nasty nuns to allow us to perform during school hours, time which should have been spent learning about St. Anthony or St. Francis and how he communicated with the little birds of Assisi. One performance in particular is indelibly etched in my mind. There was my dear sister in her blue pleated skirt and white middy blouse, coming into my classroom and, without even consulting me, asking Sister Petrina to excuse me from class for just a little while so that I could accompany her in a duet she had had me working on for several weeks. Sister Finbar, Virginia's teacher, had asked us to perform for her class.

Thinking there was nothing I could possibly do about it, I resignedly went with her to the eighth grade class, where I proceeded to sit lotus style on the floor and sing:

There's a rich Maharajah of Magadore
who has ten thousand camels or maybe more...

I sat on the floor like a yogi, moving my hands and head stiffly from left to right and right to left.

...who had rubies and pearls and the loveliest girls,
but he didn't know how to do the Rhumba.

Virginia played the slick little chick who deviously seduces the Maharajah and wipes him clean of everything. Enter Virginia, trying to be sexy:

She took his rubies and she took his pearls,
she took his camels and she took his girls...

The song did have a happy ending as

...what is more,
she took the rich Maharajah of Magadore.

At that point the slick little chick grabbed me, the Maharajah, by the arm and pulled me out of the door. The applause was embarrassing, but nowhere near as mortifying as when Virginia returned me to my class and Sister Petrina, feeling deprived because the "Andrews Sisters" had not performed for her class, insisted that I suffer the deepest humiliation by once more becoming the Maharajah of Magadore. Virginia was delighted to entertain her little sister's captive classmates.

Despite the embarrassment, I loved Virginia's plays. On rainy Saturdays when there wasn't much to do, she would make up stories that she, my cousin Evelyn, and I would act out on my mother's bed, using bedspreads as costumes. Evelyn, the cutest, was usually chosen to be queen. Virginia was always the dashing buccaneer, while my nondescript nature allowed me to develop a repertoire of roles as ladies-in-waiting, evil kings, hunchbacks, and dead people.

My parents grew increasingly concerned about the rampant drug-pushing in the neighborhood. One evening after work, my father told us that we would be moving. He had bought a house from a fellow railroad worker who was going blind and needed to relocate. I remember being excited about having my own house and especially about having a yard to play in. But how was I ever going to part with my cousins, my friends, my classmates, my neighborhood?

The fall I turned thirteen we moved to Brooklyn, an hour and a half away from the Bronx via the IRT and BMT subways—a place where people spoke funny English and rooted for a baseball team they called the Bums. My sister stopped hating me; she told me that she had always wanted to have a teen-age sister and now I finally qualified. Leaving the Bronx, I left not only the people and places I loved so much, I also traded street games, roller skating, and dolls, for boys, dances, and a new music, rock and roll.

Years later I visited my old neighborhood in the Bronx. The housing projects that replaced the razed buildings had themselves gone through some violent times and resembled pictures I had seen of war-torn Europe. The era of street vendors had come to a close; trolleys had been replaced by buses; the Gypsies had relocated to anonymous apartments. I never went back again—my childhood remains unencumbered by the present, in my memories.

Elena Harap

NELL'S EULOGY
In memory of Nell Daniels

Oh Lord, our friend is gone.
Lord, give us grandmothers like Nell!
A rock of faith,
a Christian, Nell
would never betray a friend.

Sitting in the parish office day after day, she listened
to the news on her transistor radio—racial incidents in South Boston,
police reports, government subsidies—for whom?
for her grandson, who cannot hear and speak like other children?
her young granddaughters in their starched twin Sunday dresses
and ribboned braids?

Day after day she looked upon greed, treachery and petty cruelty
that ate into her heart. Maybe she had sins of her own to hide
but all those secrets died the day Nell died.
She kept the faith.

On Sundays, dressed for church, she was as grand as any queen
and Nell could sing, and play the tambourine.
Old at fifty-two, she died too soon.
Angels lined the ridgepoles of churches in Eliot Square
crying *Lord have mercy!*
crying *Amen!*

And high above the Statehouse dome
the Saint at Heaven's gold-touched gate embraced her;
planets spun slowly in reverent welcome.

Roxbury was quiet, no one said much.
You hadn't heard? Nell Daniels died.

Now hear what I say:
Raise up your voices! Mourn and pray.
False friends betray each other every day
but Nell was loyal to us all. Amen.

Oh Lord, our friend is gone.
Lord, give us grandmothers like Nell!
Like Nell, Lord!
like
Nell.

OUTBOUND

Going through morning rituals
in the moment
before silence meets sound
María gets up at night's end
to prepare for her daily journey
in search of knowledge.

Her strength visible
to eyes that see
she stretches and yawns
before the mirror of dawn.

Inspecting the only menu
her closet offers
she chooses the red tank top
that takes shape
when it comes to rest on her breasts.
María packs cereal in a baggie
pulls a cap over yesterday's hair.

Her quick tongue wraps tightly around
words not to be spoken . . . out loud
until some wise white dude bumps
up against her in the hall.

The twenty-pound book bag
slung onto her left shoulder
tilts her unevenly toward the ground.
Saying goodbye to the Apostolic Church
and the word ZULU
painted in black on a blank wall
she boards the bus outbound.

A fellow traveler ascends at the stop
between the Full Baptist Church
and the Church of Joy and Gladness.
María knows the sun rises
over the Bodega Hispana and Smile Again Furniture.

Puerto Plata Video reflections
snap memory and fingers
as María sings *hola*
to others making this trip.

Past the West India Restaurant
Santo Domingo Street and San Juan
her head falls forward
her eyes close.

Someone told her
the answer to the dreams
that she doesn't have yet
is out there
in a place all white and green
where people live indoors
and run on million dollar playgrounds
beyond the reach
of the Perfect Truth
a full service beauty salon.

ELENA HARAP

MAGNIFICAT

Ninety-one winters rest
in the wheelchair by the wood stove.
Holding her magnifying glass by its black plastic stem,
my mother reads the comics.
She contemplates "Calvin and Hobbes";
from the opposite side of the ice-clear glass
I see a universe, a source. How she is magnified,
squinting through the lens: blue eye like lapis,
folded cheek soft as chamois cloth.
My spirit rejoices in Joan, my mother. She has filled
the hungry with good things, *esurientes implevit bonis*,
she who is mighty, *qui potens est.*
Dispersit superbos, she has scattered the proud.

She puts aside the glass, asks to go to bed.
All generations, *omnes generationes*
shall call her blessed, tuck blankets warm
along her back, rub her smooth feet.
The reading glass lies ready by a book
on the bedside table,
in case she should wake in the night.

BLANCA BONILLA

¿QUIÉN ERES TÚ?/WHO ARE YOU?

Note: Iris is the fourth child in my family. As a little girl she had long, curly hair and big green eyes; she was always smiling. My parents said that she loved to sing and dance. She received compliments everywhere she went. At the age of three she had polio.

Her life in Puerto Rico was not easy; there were not many opportunities for handicapped children. She walked with crutches, but that did not stop her from wanting to excel. At eighteen she moved to Boston with our family. She was determined to learn English. She listened to American music, read every day, and practiced. Three months later she was translating for everybody in the family. She was the first in the family to obtain a driver's license and the first to graduate from college.

Iris is my sister; she has been a role model for all of us.

Nacida bajo el nombre de Grismilda
conocida entre sus hermanos como Mirta
admirada por sus amigos como Iris
y adorada por su compañero como Millie.

Mujer de ojos verdes
los más hermosos que he podido contemplar
su mirada cambia dependiendo del
personaje que va a jugar.

Grismilda, la doncella que borró de sus pensamientos
la que le dió sufrimientos
en este mundo a veces tan injusto
en este mundo a veces tan eterno.

Mirta, la que disfrutó de su familia
la que reía y jugaba
la que creía en luchar
sin ver los obstáculos para poder lograr.

Iris, coqueta amada por muchos hombres
mujer dueña de su vida
madre independiente y liberada
vive la vida como es debido.
Millie, la princesa judía

la que no cela ni envidia
protegida y mimada
por su esposo día por día.

¿Cuál es mi hermana
Grismilda, Mirta, Iris o Millie?
Sencillamente, es una combinación
de estos personajes que lleva en su corazón.

Born under the name of *Grismilda*
known among her siblings as *Mirta*
admired by her friends as *Iris*
and adored by her partner as *Millie*.

Woman with green eyes,
the most beautiful that I have contemplated
her gaze changes depending on
the character she is going to play.

Grismilda, the damsel that she erased from her thoughts
the one that gave her sorrows
in this world sometimes so unjust
in this world sometimes so unending.

Mirta, she who enjoyed her family
the one who laughed and played
the one who believed in struggling
ignoring the obstacles so that she could reach the goal.

Iris, coquette, loved by many men
owner of her life
mother independent and liberated
living life as it should be lived.

Milllie, the Jewish princess
neither jealous nor envious
protected and indulged
by her husband day by day.

Which one is my sister?
Grismilda, Mirta, Iris, or Millie?
Simply, it's a combination
of these roles she carries in her heart.

Elena Harap

RESTORATION CREW AT THE BURIAL GROUND
Putney, Vermont, 1993

They are tending the graveyard,
propping up history's thin stones
knocked askew by falling trees, rain, wind,
frost heaves. They are careful not to disturb
the bones. Sweating and bending, they reset
each marker. *Abiah Foster, Age 61.*
Charlotte, wife of Israel Hodgkin,
died in her 36th year. Lucy, daughter of
Persis & Wilder Aplin.

                         Mosquitoes
attack from the surrounding woods;
one must mow, cut brush, rebuild the stone wall,
sow grass that grows in shade. Arched stones
like doors, vertical and plumb once more,
admit their guests. *Carmelita, Artemas, Thomas;*
safely home. In glorious hope this sleeping dust
from pain and suffering free. Their memory is blessed.

This work never ends, only the workers come and go.
Emerging from stone-dust and rot
they laugh and ignore their nettle stings.
In the company of *Jonas, died age 15*
and *Mary, wife of Maynard Perry, AEt. 88*
they have acquired knowledge: *seedtime and harvest*
shall not cease—a plain mystery
they will carry to their own graves.

Li Min Mo

A BUNDLE OF LAUNDRY NOTES

A round the corner from our tenement building in Little Italy, New York, I saw a storefront sign with Chinese ideograms painted in red over a black background: Hand Laundry. I had lived here for only a couple of months and was thrilled to find a Chinese neighbor. Peeking into the shop, I saw an old man bending over his counter, writing with a Chinese brush. What was he writing? To whom? That lonesome portrait struck a chord in me; stranded eight thousand miles away from home, he had nothing to turn to except his brush, ink, and paper. The tiny storefront was yellowed by years of dust and the heat from all the ironing. Behind the counter, stacks of laundry were neatly tucked into their compartments. Against one wall, coats, gowns, and folded bedspreads hung from a metal rack.

I went home and told my mother about the shop; she threw a fit. "Don't you ever go into that dingy place. That man is an embarrassment to us Chinese, washing ocean devils' dirty underwear and socks . . . that's the lowest job. What a shame!" I didn't say anything. Her resentment spurred my curiosity. Deep down, I understood her outrage—it reflected how she felt about her own place. An acclaimed writer and journalist in China, now she had to toil in sweatshops.

For years she took on many jobs—scrubbing toilets in the Chinese movie theatre, waitressing in a tiny twenty-four-hour café. Eventually she went back to school, became a laboratory technician, and years later earned a master's degree in Chinese literature. There was an indomitable spirit in her, a desire to learn, to improve herself, to gain knowledge. The love of education was instilled in us by her example. She didn't want her kids to pursue things that she felt were just a waste of time.

One day, filled with curiosity, I disobeyed my mother and walked into the Hand Laundry shop. Smells of ammonia and bleach permeated the air. I tried my poor Cantonese on the owner. It turned out he understood only Toisanese. He laughed at my tentative words and mumbled something, revealing yellow crooked teeth. A dark brown, twiggy, diminutive man, he wore his shirt unbuttoned, sleeves rolled up to the elbows, and underneath a worn-out tee shirt. A sash held up his dark pants. I watched him going to the back of the storefront into a narrow bathroom. A double hot plate was propped up over the tank of the toilet; he poured himself a glass of tea. I noticed some chicken wings with ginger stewing in a pot.

Chinese people don't introduce themselves the way the Western do. I never learned the old hand-laundry-man's name. After a few short visits to his shop, I lost interest; I was busy with homework, movies, and daydreaming about how great life would be in high school.

Several years later, it surprised me to find the laundry shop closed. The storefront on Broome Street had been boarded up. The old man must have passed away and left a pile of ocean devils' dirty laundry. I knew only a little about him. In his teens he had immigrated to America with his uncle, looking for gold; he was a hard-working, little-talk man. He must have tried to get in touch with his family in China. American immigration law barred Chinese laborers from bringing their wives and children to the States. In a land filled with spirits he didn't know, writing with the brush was his sole connection to his homeland. I walked away, thinking about his unfinished notes, how he had labored over the back of the laundry labeling paper with his brush; the pink sheets were living membranes, spirit paper. He worked quickly, the tip of his brush like the point of a ballet shoe, seizing the moment, levitated suddenly by an image. His graceful "grass style" brush work looked like breath dancing, dark flowing motions riding out into a cloud.

It took years, I knew, to gain control of the brush, keep the wrist steady, and move with the bone of the word. My mother had made me practice with the brush for years, and she told me even the "wild form"—an eccentric style, difficult to decipher—contained a universe of its own. More than three decades afterwards, I learned to write in English and developed my own voice. The old laundry man, whom I named Old Wing, appeared in my stories. I created the Wing family, who lived on Mott Street around the corner from the hand laundry shop. Old Wing's step-granddaughter Carol became the narrator.

was away in college and rarely got home to visit, but that spring I went to see my mother. Some people were taking down the sign above the door of Old Wing's laundry. My mother walked out with boxes and bundles under her arms.

"Mom, what's going on here?" I asked. "Do you need some help?" Joyce's face was solemn, stiff; her newly permed hair looked artificial and wig-like. I went into the laundry shop. The tiny storefront was lit by a bright fluorescent bulb. Everything was in disarray—boxes of old clothes piled high against the wall, shoe boxes stacked on top of the narrow, tall, wooden counter. A large rack of clean, unclaimed clothes in their plastic covers hung next to the counter. The shelves along the wall behind it were bare and dusty. It seemed to me the shop had not been in operation for quite some time.

Joyce was unusually tight-mouthed that afternoon. I wouldn't push her to talk when she was in that kind of mood. I helped her lug some boxes upstairs to her apartment. Old Yang, Old Wing's best friend, showed up to lend us a hand, and Old Wing's sister-in-law, Fungjie, came too, with her daughter Julie. We piled up most of the boxes and pressed clothes in the hall.

"What are you going to do with all this stuff?" Fungjie asked, putting down a big pile of dirty laundry in the hallway.

"I think I'll bag it and throw it out. It's no use to anyone," Mother said, going into the kitchen to wash her hands at the sink. I looked at Old Yang, sitting next to the window and opening a thermos, pouring himself a cup of tea.

"Old Yang, what happened to Old Wing, is he still at the hospital?"

Old Yang, the calmest of us all, stroked his white beard. "Old Wing passed away three months ago. In the old country we have to mourn for three years, but your mom is following the new custom. Three months is up and she is disbanding the shop and throwing away the old man's stuff."

Fungjie turned to him. "What old tradition? This is America. Finally we can take down the sign and clean up the place. We respected the old man. He was in the hospital for almost a year and we never touched a thing in his shop. We want to turn it into a clothing alteration shop. There's a lot of room in the back."

"Fungjie, stop dreaming. Where are we going to get the money for a new shop?" Mother lamented. She sat down on a chair, looking through an old shoe box she had brought up from the laundry.

"Didn't the old man leave you some of his savings?" Fungjie asked as she sorted through a pile of old clothes.

"How many times do I have to tell you, that old fool left us a debt, three months of unpaid rent, and all this garbage." Mother sounded angry. "Old Yang, look at this bundle of old paper; tell me, what kind of writing is this? I bet it's nothing important." Joyce had grown up poor in China and never learned to read or write Chinese. After immigrating to America, she had gone to high school and earned a diploma. As she handed over the whole box to Old Yang, she muttered indignantly, "That old man spent all his money on this prostitute on Mott Street. He left me not a dime toward his own burial." She picked up another old shoe box. I thought she might be looking for money the old man had stashed away.

"Tzahong,"—Old Yang preferred to call my mother by her Chinese name, Colorful Rainbow—"you shouldn't bad-mouth my best friend; besides, he is your step-father. Let him rest in peace. He provided for your mother and you when you first came to Gold Mountain. It took him twenty years to save up that money to get a wife." And he added, "Young Wing and I will try to get some money to help you."

I could never get the story straight from my mother about Old Wing's relationship to us. Later I learned from Fungjie that my grandmother was his paper-wife and indentured servant or slave. He spent six thousand dollars to buy this wife, who insisted on bringing along her daughter. From the age of twelve, my mother had worked with her mother as a seamstress in a sweatshop. According to tradition, she was supposed to take care of Old Wing until he died. Indentured slaves. My mother was ashamed of that position and that's why she refused to reveal the truth to me. My dad, a co-owner of a small bookstore in Chinatown, never got along with my grandfather; he didn't want to have anything to do with the old man. I knew Fungjie was a paper-bride brought to America by Old Wing's younger brother, Ken Wing. She didn't hide that fact from anyone; she felt proud that by being sold to Ken Wing she had helped her family in Hong Kong.

"Hey, this is not garbage. These are poems Old Wing wrote. First-rate grass-style calligraphy!" exclaimed Old Yang, placing some worn strips of paper on the kitchen table. He was overwhelmed with joy and sadness as he read aloud Old Wing's poetry. Many times he burst into tears. I hadn't studied hard in Chinese school, but I recognized some characters and could understand a few Toisanese phrases. Fungjie translated the poems into English for me.

> To Fay-Yen—Flying Swallow:
> When I eat tangerines,
> sip Dragon Well,
> stare into the lone eye of a goldfish,
> I think of you,
> in a dark room,
> on Mott Street.
> Moon face, starry eyes,
> cherry mouth,
> light peal of laughter.
> Your hand delicately fingered,
> a blue-flowered porcelain cup
> emptying Dragon Well.
> Weaving another hand in the air
> you sing-song talk about the joy of three goldfish.
>
> The red thread of love—
> on a full moon's night
> an invisible red thread
> tied together our wrists,
> our souls, our next life.
> I knew a kind of love, then,
> supple as silk threads,
> earthly like babies' breath,
> delicately forceful like
> the lush tremblings of the first
> sighted colors of spring,
> And your singing,
> shrill ringing cadences,
> fluttering in my hands.

Hearing these poems, Joyce grumbled, "My old mother was right about that dirty old man." Throwing a scornful look at Old Yang, she dumped the shoe box on the floor and left the kitchen. I leaned over the table and studied the thin strips of paper, yellow at the edges. Old Wing used to label his customers' laundry with them. They reminded me of menus of house specials tacked on walls in Chinese restaurants. Examining them more closely, I felt there was something in the strips—strokes of ink were dashed on quickly, light coming through Old Wing's tired, dark, lonesome hours.

Old Yang was wiping tears out of his eyes with the back of his hand. "For years Old Wing tried in vain to locate his family in Southwestern China. Finally he received a note that informed him his village had been completely decimated. All that was left was a barren hill. The people who used to live there must have escaped to other parts of China."

We didn't know that, for Old Wing hadn't shown grief to us or talked about his family in China. When I was last home, a year ago, Old Wing was already sickly. He was in and out of the hospital a lot, and Mother always complained about how hard she had to work in maintaining both his shop and her seamstress job. He was a frail little guy, I remembered, with dark circles around his big eyes, and a bald spot on the center of his head. He would nod with his eyes closed when I talked to him, and on some occasions, when I used to go to his shop as a kid, to drop some things for Joyce, he would offer me a red envelope with ten dollars in it, and Chinese sesame candy or almond cookies. One time I noticed that his long, bony fingers were almost bleached white, a sharp contrast with his dark, speckled arms. The image of those fingers of his haunted me in my dreams.

Old Yang cleared his throat and drank another sip of tea. "Old Wing wasn't himself after he got that news, twenty-two years ago, about his village. I think he had been waiting for years for the ancient Wing spirits to take him back to China."

I pulled out another strip of poetry and asked Old Yang to decipher the words for us. The paper looked new. The translation went like this:

No-name river: I wake up crying these days like a child.
Men are supposed to be strong, unshakeable,
forever mountains.
Now women's sorrow runs in my blood
and my life is a no-name river.

I got the news that our old village
is just a barren hill.
The news rattles me like a powerful gale.
My life is tossing in the merciless storm,
my heart a torn mast,
my vision a broken compass.

Old Wing's poetry made me sad and connected me to my grandparents' past. As I was fond of calligraphy, I asked Mother and Old Yang if I might take those notes and study them. No one objected; they gave me three shoe boxes full of Old Wing's laundry notes. I'm an art major and a western style painter. The Chinese grass-style calligraphy reminded me of Jackson Pollock's paintings. The rapid, spontaneous movement of the ink was like strokes of flight bursting into being. Old Wing had spilled out his thoughts onto the paper, not for his own comfort; they were meant for his family. Eight thousand miles away there might be one person still wishing to know his well-being. And Old Wing's words had not died.

For a month I went down to Chinatown three times a week, hung out with Old Yang in Lucky Café with some of his coffee-shop friends, and listened to their translation of Old Wing's poetry. Like scientists finding a dinosaur bone by accident, we all were excited. We cheered each one's effort when a whole phrase was deciphered. It was like trying to repair lost pigment on an old painting.

Old Yang usually commented sadly after each new translation, "I truly share Old Wing's sentiments. It's like the world has forgotten about you, and your life is a living mystery. Aiii! What's keeping you alive? Is that fate?" To me the calligraphy ink was Old Wing's blood, still flowing. Its bare symbols were wild dances challenging me to explore my heritage, and life in America in the early 1900's. The strips, torn and filled with moth holes, unfolded a story.

*   *   *

Many moons, grape picking. Blood of fruit runs deep into my own, vines cut my fingers. My back twisted, pained, carrying so many baskets. Sky naked, blue, hot, and silent. They press wine out of these red fruits. Drinks grace the tables I never sit around. I know the taste, aged like my body, bitter like my sorrow. Rain, sun, earth, fertilizer, and sweat purified. Many hands' labor and then bottled. The more I work here, the more bottles appear in my dreams. One day I took off, drunk with new visions.

Seattle, rain, greens everywhere. Apple orchard work. Hard, sweet, climb many trees. Pick until my hands turn apple. My eyes see red bobbing. Too many bushels. One big fall. Getting too old for the tree tops. Little money. Long train rides. Many dreams. Try to catch some. Always running away. Still want to be a boy. Foolish thoughts. I sing loud opera with the train whistling through the tunnels.

Kansas City. Dust flying. I want to cry. Too flat. No business. One small hand laundry. People not friendly. Call names. Looks scary to be here. Chinese man can be in trouble here. One red man, friendly, brings his shirts to cousin Pang. We make jokes. "Yellow man and red man make the white man look more pale, but deadly." No money or gold here. Just open space. One can see the edge of the world. Bleak. No colors like Seattle. Miss the mountain, trees, ocean.

Aboard the train to New York. Great view opens my heart, see vast America, many spirits, many lost men like me. In the dark I get scared. More rides, more open country, less heart to go on. Still young. Tired. Twenty years not long to search for gold. If I have magic, I'll turn into a big rock and sit in the bottom of the Grand Canyon. Let the wind, rain, sun shape me again. This time better fit for this barbaric place. What is a good man if he cannot stretch his vision beyond the horizon, work hard from sunrise to sunset, build a fortune for offspring?

Oh my family, it's not that I have not tried. Misfortune befalls me. This is the White Men's world. They don't want me to be here, to learn a trade, to own a piece of land. They brought us here to break a strike in California. They tricked us. We thought we were going to Gold Mountain to dig gold. Then the striking workers beat us, killed some, chased us out of town. Maybe I was lucky. Still have a life ahead. But what kind of life? Sometimes I just want to die and go join the dead ones. Then I hear my ancestor's voice: "Never take a son's life into your own hand." One of them is watching me. One day my luck will change.

No incense. I use cigarette butts when I pray and share my food with gods. Sometimes no food for the whole day, no wine; then I share my saliva with gods. I can beg for cigarettes. Smoking is bad for my cough. When I light one, I see my familiar village. Rising smoke.

Chicago, a cousin rides in my car. Old Yang, younger, stronger, happier man. Very happy. We are from the same city, different village. He's rich. Gold watch, nice clothes, shining shoes, gold teeth, and Cuban cigars. He runs a business in Florida and

Cuba. He asked me to go. I declined. No more orchard work for me. My cousin from San Francisco just opened a café in New York Chinatown. We exchanged addresses.

New York City, five years I wait at tables, wash the floor, make signs for shops, "No smoking, drinking, or gambling." I want to open my own business. I feel young again. All the years of bitterness not gone but set aside. If my family joins me, I'll try to live for a long time.

My brother Young Wing just arrived from Philadelphia after he had a big fight with his restaurant owner. He is looking for work as a cook. If he does not find a job, I told him I will share my business with him. Just three rules at home and shop. No drinking. No white women at night. No gambling on the holidays. I am still the oldest son and boss here.

These have been good years. Working for myself. I feel proud. The laundry business is good and we have both saved a lot of money. Young Wing wants a beautiful young Hong Kong girl.

After ten years Old Yang appeared in front of my business. Weaker and lost everything. Never try to tell the future. It's tricky.

No more dreams. Just the coming and going of weak breaths. No more questions or visions of why this or how come that. The centering force is gone. What's left is a small hope like the faint light of the lighthouse spotted in a storm, in the misty rain. Some day someone will read these brush strokes.

Weak back, sore, calloused hands. No good working man. Gold is deep. Do I have the strength?

ELENA HARAP

SHE PRAYS

Aholiday visit to an old friend with whom I lived in Boston during a crucial period of my adolescence reveals a quiet lesson in aging and discipline. I first met Bertha as a student volunteer in a Quaker project offering household help to families in the mostly Catholic and working class neighborhood of Mission Hill. A longtime neighborhood resident in her middle forties, Bertha lived in a brick row house built in the 1870s, when streetcar lines began to link Boston neighborhoods with downtown and with the furniture factories, meat packing plants, and breweries that rose up at the edges of the growing city. The house stood on a street near the bottom of the hill, just around the corner from the tall stone towers of the Church of Our Lady of Perpetual Help. It was a hard time; her husband was missing, no word for some months, and she was working as a charwoman, struggling to keep the family going. Our student crew put a fresh coat of paint on her front parlor—a high-ceilinged, pleasant room with curtained bow windows looking out on the street; got acquainted with the boisterous family of seven sons and one daughter, and came back later to visit over cups of tea.

The Mission Church, its familiar name, was the center of a community: library, butcher shop, religious store, bakery, municipal building with its gymnasium for the young people and welfare offices for the poor. There was a convent and a priests' residence; the sisters in particular were a presence on the street, in full, dark habits, faces framed in starched white. It was 1959 and nuns had not yet been permitted to switch to ordinary street dress. I was a privileged college kid with a scholarship and a family who loved and had high hopes for me, but in my last year the pressure became too great and I ran; I ran to Bertha's house, with its cracked plaster, children's initials carved into the wooden posts at the landings of its four stories, kitchen in the basement cluttered with family-sized boxes of Corn Flakes and piles of laundry. Bertha welcomed me in, making space for me in a small back room on the top floor, looking toward the double stone towers of the church. After a year as a big sister in that household, working at a nearby hospital and rethinking my choices, I went back to college and graduated. By then I had been thoroughly adopted, an honorary member of their family, the children told me. Almost forty years later, now with a family of my own, I enter Bertha's home expecting and getting an unconditional welcome.

But in the 1990s she lives alone. Her husband, who did come back, has died and the children have scattered to the suburbs, raising smaller families than hers in two-story houses with green yards. She has left the old neighborhood for a one-bedroom subsidized apartment in a development south of the central city, still urban but without the beehive of small streets and places of business that characterized Mission Hill. A major highway runs nearby, a large Walgreen's Drug replaces the corner store. The energy that took her shopping on Saturdays for bargains among the wagons at Haymarket and faithfully to early Mass every day is focused inward now, concentrated on the apparently limited world she occupies in these few scrupulously clean, very warm rooms. The living room is a panorama of Christmas cards jostling on the mantelpiece, glass-fronted cabinet, tables, and shelves. The usual photos of grandchildren, which I study in order to keep current with the family's evolution, are obscured by cards and well-wishings. A holiday bouquet I ordered from the florist sits awkward and out-of-scale in a large, blossom-shaped glass dish, but Bertha displays it in the middle of her round formica-topped table, not even removing the desiccated lilies going limp and transparent among perky red carnations and white chrysanthemums. The promised festive arrangement in a crystal bowl turns out to be a mismatched collection of flowers, gaudy gold-sprayed cherubs, and silver pine cones, with two red tapers sticking up like unlit street lamps, their wicks still in plastic sleeves—she hasn't burned them, perhaps feeling this bouquet is so foreign it should not be touched. Beside it sits a much prettier, smaller cluster of flowers from one of her grandsons. Never mind. This room is large enough for whatever offerings arrive.

Bertha sits in her Christmas house and welcomes my husband and me as always, confessing that she is about three inches shorter than the five-foot-two she used to be and hardly has strength in her hands for crocheting the generous output of blankets and baby clothes she once supplied to family and friends. She has arthritis in her hip and does very little walking: a weekly trip to the grocery store with her daughter and, once in a while, a family party or a christening. So now her work is to pray. Two rosaries in the morning before going into the shower. Then prayers to Padre Pio, her favorite saint; she shows us his picture, the oval solemn face and dark hair framed in a cardboard holder standing on the television set. After she gets dressed, she watches a mass on TV and says another rosary. Sometimes there is a sermon by a television priest. She might say a rosary in the afternoon.

"I can't do very much, so I might as well do that," she says, realistic as ever, of her morning schedule. "Big Bertha," friends used to tease her, and the broad body in its flowered house dress is still firm and comforting. She reaches up to hug us, the tall, pushing-sixty generation, and lets us hug her back. I feel her fine white hair against my cheek. I offer to heat water for tea, seeing that even to get up and fill the pot sitting ready on the clean stovetop is an effort, noting how she has placed a loaf of homemade banana bread from the freezer, wrapped in foil, to thaw on the counter in readiness for this occasion.

"I can't eat banana bread myself, but I make it for everybody who comes to visit. They all seem to like it," she explains. In the last few years she has given up sugar to control diabetes—another discipline she learns and practices in old age, a serious renunciation it seems to me, when I remember the sugar bowl that always sat on her kitchen table, the many cups of sweetened tea we drank, the bags of cookies close at hand—muddy black Hydrox, an imitation Oreo cookie which the children liked, while I preferred the macaroons, colored pink and green, that she would buy in bulk at the market. Banana bread is Bertha's specialty, however, and now she has plenty of time to bake it, for others to eat.

We talk over family news: triumph of a grandchild born with Downs' Syndrome, now graduated from high school and holding a job, sadness for a divorced son struggling to make a home in which to nurture his five-year-old daughter, pieces of information about each life, a personal rosary spilling through the conversation, interrupted by moments of memory and reflection.

"I have learned not to let things upset me too much," Bertha tells us. "After all, what can I do?" But we know that she absorbs all the pain and longing and exhilaration, eighty years gathered into her beads and ceremoniously paid out, morning and evening between arthritic fingers, like the line of an anchor. The beads are heavy, heavy, bearing the heart of a living woman, the unsacred heart, shaped by German Meiningers on her mother's side and Irish Roses on her father's, by marriage to her soldier beau in wartime, by motherhood, eight children, twenty-one grandchildren, by widowhood—and by an innate quality of loyalty to friends, not without bursts of temper and recrimination, but always returning to acceptance, always to remembrance of us in her prayers.

This is so extraordinary, so surprising to me, that someone in an unpretentious set of rooms—full of doily-bedecked chairs and tables, a menagerie of stuffed animals for grandchildren to play with, wedding pictures hung in a frieze of white dresses and self-conscious smiles, satin-robed plaster saints with bland, compassionate eyes—someone here is praying for the well-being of my family. Daily and specifically. I myself, raised a Protestant, do not pray and wish blessings for her as faithfully as she does for me; but I will go and sit in Bertha's circle of working prayer. As awkward as my oversized arrangement of flowers are my attempts to pray, asking the guidance of an unknown power, surrounding with light the faces of people I love, repeating to myself words of psalms from Sunday School in a Southern church basement with a dark red painted cement floor and a wheezy portable organ, or from summer camp outdoor services on a rocky, wooded point in Maine. *How precious also are thy thoughts unto me, O God, how great is the sum of them.*

That sum I can almost begin to comprehend when I confront Bertha's daily occupation, the sacred words, unoriginal, marking days and years, the accompanying attention to individuals living their harlequin lives. There is a spiritual lesson here, I sense more than perceive it. Out of her own stubborn humility my friend has achieved, or always had, a truly gracious presence. It seems that pure luck—could that be the blessing of God?—has put a teacher before me. I recall all the formulas with which Bertha makes small split-second rituals in response to everyday departures, complaints, and fears. Be careful and be good. Patience is a virtue; have a little. The good Lord never sends you anything you can't handle. The last, the oldest one, she gives us as we go out from the small white-painted and Christmas card-papered apartment, out to see how we might practice a discipline inspired by hers—"Goodbye and God bless."

BLANCA BONILLA

VIVIR/TO LIVE

Hoy voy a hacer que el cielo me vista de sorpresas misteriosas
que el sol me alumbre mis caminos y me guíe
que las estrellas se apoderen de mis deseos y anhelos
y que la luna me arrope con su manto.
Hoy, es un día especial . . . ¡Siento mi espíritu vibrar!

Today I am going to make the sky dress me with mysterious surprises
the sun brighten my paths and direct me
the stars take power over my desires and longings
and the moon wrap me in its mantle.
Today is a special day . . . I feel my spirit vibrate!

Mu Shi/Mother Stream

BLANCA BONILLA

PARA MI MADRE/FOR MY MOTHER

Que mujer luminosa
Hermosa . . . como una rosa
Limpia . . . como el agua del río
Humilde y tranquila . . .
Como un pichón en su ni'o

María, hembra completa
Rubia, blanca y sensual
Su mirada penetra
Como una medalla de seguridad
Su devoción a su familia
Es de mil una en la sociedad

Es millonaria en alegrías
Alivia mis tristezas
Esta gran mujer está disponible
En las malas y en las buenas

No tiene precio mi madre
Es un tesoro total
Dios, bendiga a mi viejita
Que hoy la quiero aún más

Dedicada a tu hogar
Te enfrentastes a los retos
De los campesinos pobres
Con orgullo y con empeño

En temprana edad
Aprendistes a sembrar
A colar el café
Y defenderte pa' un hornar

Jíbara, hembra,
Eres tú madre mía
Renunciastes tus fantasías
Para ser madre todos los días

Cantan los ruiseñores
Al verte todos los días
Te dan la bienvenida
Y la bendición del día
Le pedías a las estrellas
Que del cielo se caían
Sin ver los resultados
Creías día por día

Vivías el presente
Esperabas un buen porvenir
Enseñabas a tus hijos
La doctrina de vivir

Madre mereces un premio
Un premio que reconozcan
Que engendrastes trece hijos
Y los guiastes hacia adelante
Asegurándoles vidas sanas
Sin rubíes ni diamantes

María Veléz de Bonilla,
La dama que me parió
Señora sabia y astuta
La mujer que admiro yo

What a luminous woman
Gorgeous . . . like a rose
Pure . . . as the water of the river
Humble and serene . . .
As a young bird in its nest

María, fulfilled woman
Blonde, fair-skinned, and sensuous
Her look protects
Like a medal of security
Her devotion to the family
Is unequaled in society

She is a millionaire in joys
Alleviates my sorrows
This great woman is available
In bad times and good times

My mother has no price
She is a perfect treasure
God bless my dear old one
Whom I love even more today

Dedicated to your household
You confronted the challenges
Of poor peasants
With pride and commitment

At an early age
You learned to sow seed
To brew coffee
To provide for our needs

Puerto Rican, female
You are, my mother
You renounced your fantasies
To be a mother every day

The nightingales sing
As they see you every day
They give you their welcome
And the blessing of the day
You wished on stars
That shot down the sky
Without seeing the results
You kept believing day by day

You lived the present
Hoped for a better future
You taught your children
The doctrine of living

Mother, you deserve an award
A prize that recognizes

How you birthed thirteen children
And guided them forward
Assuring them healthy lives
Without rubies or diamonds

María Veléz de Bonilla,
The woman who gave birth to me
Señora, astute and wise
The *doña* I admire

LI MIN MO

WHAT FAY-YEN CARRIES
ACROSS THE PACIFIC

She has to smuggle red beans of love,
long-life potions, swallow's-nest soup,
blood-strengthening roots, Dragon Well tea.

Mornings at her village market
she will carry on board:
fresh spices, baby orchids, gardenias,
lush wet greens, red lichees, golden melons,
peasants hauling, hum and sigh of their muscles,
songs of fortune tellers' caged canaries,
trails of sandalwood smoke,
hands shaping lotuses, moving lips of mantras,
brown soles of worshipers, swaying backs
at the Earth Goddess Temple.

Into the bamboo trunk she puts
a carefully rolled-up thousand-year scroll:
the spirited sights of a festival,
splendid Dragon Boats,
rowers' forceful arms, drummers on the helms,
the cheering crowd like countless waving flags,
enthusiasm of a hot summer
celebrating words of the great poet Ch'u Yuan,
"I sport with you
by the Nine Rivers."

The last thing she packs:
a green silk sash,
the one that was washed
in the river of her childhood,
so she will be able to tie
her soul to the source when she dies.

Mary Millner McCullough

ORIS AND THE HAIR THING

Oris sat in the spare room, her head imprisoned under the hood of the hair dryer. Her scalp fought a major battle with the tight plastic rollers around which she had twisted her hair. She felt as if her pores were giving birth to millions of tiny insects. She was getting ready for the banquet planned in honor of her husband, Russell, that same evening. Oris wanted to look attractive, to be a credit to Russell. It was important.

Damn, be honest with yourself. You know you want to look sexy and beautiful, she thought. Looks had always been important to her. She planned to wear an electric blue dress that made her chocolate-kissed skin look radiant, accenting her curves in all the right places. Russell would approve. Looking good, especially when she was with Russell, was written between the lines of their marriage contract. What to do with her hair was the problem she was trying to solve. She tried not to think about being the only black woman at the dinner as she revisited the argument she had had with Russell at the dinner table the night before.

"O," Russell had said, calling her by his special nickname as he licked the chicken leg he held to his lips, "don't forget we have the banquet at the University tomorrow night." Oris had been looking forward to doing nothing on Saturday evening. She had planned to do some house chores and spend the evening with the mystery she was in the middle of reading. Working ten-hour days non-stop at school for almost a month now had left her with little energy to pay attention to Russell or anything else. She felt used up. Going out Saturday evening meant doing something about her hair, another chore to add to the Saturday list.

Oris took a deep breath and straightened her shoulders, realizing that she would once more go along to get along. "So who'll be there?"

"Professors Watts, Burn, Jalen, and their wives, and all the non-tenured faculty, of course. I invited some of the graduate students from my classes," Russell replied.

Pushing her chair back, Oris started clearing the table and asking the questions whose answers she already knew. "Any African Americans?"

"Why do we have to go through this every time I ask you to do something with me at the University? You know that I am the only black professor in the department. There are no black graduate students. There's one Asian and one Arab, both males, in my classes. There's one young woman of mixed race—African and white, I think—in Professor Watts' class. Our African American student enrollment is a disappointment to everyone. That's why we formed the diversity committee. The new president has recruitment of qualified minorities at the top of his list of priorities."

Oris watched the hot water run over the dishes she had placed in the sink. "Shame on you, Russell. I can't believe you used the word *qualified*."

Russell's eyes narrowed behind the thick, dark-rimmed glasses. "Why are you picking at this now?"

Reaching into the sink, Oris pulled the sponge from under a food-encrusted plate and squeezed the excess water out of it. "I am not picking at anything, Russell. I don't hear you referring to 'qualified' white students in your graduate seminar. Everyone assumes that whites are qualified. It's a code, Russell, a bigot's code word. Doesn't it make you angry?" Oris could feel her breath squeezing out through her nostrils, making her voice sound grating and harsh.

Walking to the refrigerator, Russell reached for a beer. Oris watched him as he gulped the beer down. "I thought you were giving up beer."

"I changed my mind." Russell reached for a second beer.

Oris loaded the dishwasher and wiped off the table. Russell sat watching her. He always hung around until she finished in the kitchen. He enjoyed watching her as she moved around the kitchen, putting it in order. He once confided that his favorite place for doing his homework as a boy had been at the kitchen table after dinner while his mother washed the dishes.

"I am tired of being the only black woman at your parties."

"And I'm tired of hearing you say it." Russell got up, then sat back down. "Tell you what, this is the last faculty party. No need to go to any more after this one. Just one favor. Tomorrow, don't get into any discussions about affirmative action with the dean."

Oris knew she would continue to attend Russell's faculty parties and they would continue to fight over who was not hired to teach and the lack of students of color in his classes. It was a crime that so few young black students would experience his brilliance as a teacher.

"Oh, well," she sighed into the room as she again tried to concentrate on her book. She wondered how many of the other wives started getting ready twelve hours in advance of the actual event. Her hair was not easy to get under control. It took lots of work and many combinations of creams to get it anywhere near manageable.

Oris put down her book and reached for the hair styling magazine for black women, placed within reach before she had sat down under the dryer. She turned the pages, looking for the one perfect style. It had to be one that she could recreate. Having studied the hairdos on the white models in other magazines, she knew it was futile to try to copy those styles. Those models were mostly blondes and had straight hair. There was often one token black model who looked like a white model with a suntan. It was hard to tell what kind of hair the alleged black model had because the hair was always straight, pulled to one side of her face with a hair clip. The models had the same straight nose, no lips, and no hips. They looked like boys in dresses to her.

The hairstyles in black hair magazines for people like her were elaborate weaves shaped like bird nests or baskets. Some looked like wings expanding from the side of the model's head. When Oris looked closely at one particular black model's hair, she was certain the hair had been frightened straight with chemicals. It stood out from the woman's head like toothpicks in an orange. Oris wanted an elegant, no-frills hairstyle that was easy, manageable, and would last more than a second.

If only I had the guts to stop this hair thing. Does my liberation mean a bald head? She thought of her son's girlfriend, replaying the image of Lauren sitting in the living room chair on Friday evening, her hair flowing like water from the kitchen faucet down her back to her butt. Someone in the room had said, "Lauren, your hair is really getting long." Lauren had responded by wrapping one hand around the hair at the back of her neck, then throwing her head towards her knees and sweeping her hair up over her head. Her free hand tied the hair into a knot. Oris had watched the movement of hands, hair, and head. Lauren seemed to move as if swimming in a heavy liquid. Her impulse to say, "Don't tie your hair into knots," had stuck in her throat. Lauren's hair was not likely to get tangled. Images flashed before Oris of all the times she had struggled with her daughter as she dragged a comb that resembled a miniature rake through her hair to remove the knots. Lauren's hair-flipping and knot-tying almost made her say something nice to Lauren about her hair, but the moment passed.

Lauren announced to the room, "I am so tired of this. I am going to cut it off, really, really short." No one saw the sneer that appeared on Oris' face. *Why do all these young white girls say "really, really,"* she wondered. Oris struggled with her desire to slap the squeak out of Lauren's voice when she talked in that silly way. The hostility Lauren's words evoked had nothing to do with Lauren. She had grown fond of the young woman as she had gotten to know her. Oris could see the wholeness of Lauren, the person, and her whiteness. Oris recognized that it was the hair thing again.

Lauren had talked on and on, providing details about her hair problems, the bad cuts and the wrong tints. Oris listened. She moved closer, even touching Lauren's hair, but she could not see what Lauren described. Lauren's hair always looked very presentable and attractive. The oiliness meant she just needed to wash it more often. Oris' hair, on the other hand, was a different story. It always needed a good greasing. It *never* looked the same, no matter what she did to it. On rare occasions her hair might look as she wanted it—but like dew on morning grass, perfection was fleeting.

Oris had tested all the promises of the right shampoos and conditioners. For years, before going to bed she had followed the same steps to prepare her hair for the next day. First she applied ample amounts of Ultra Sheen; then she parted the hair into small sections and wrapped the small portions of hair onto store-bought blue plastic rollers. Like blue-uniformed roly-poly soldiers in formation, the rollers marched up one side of her head and down the other. Then she tied an old rag around her head to hold the rollers in place. One blue soldier always went AWOL to Russell's side of the bed. There it would hide under Russell's back as he lay sleeping beside her. The next morning, Russell would rise from the bed with the roller in his hand and a look on his face. He didn't need words to communicate his displeasure as he insisted that she massage his sore back.

With all her careful work, strands of hair always managed to take flight like bats at sundown. One side always looked shorter than the other. None of the styles she tried to copy ever turned out the way they looked in the magazines. Russell wanted to know why she didn't go to a professional hair salon. They could afford it. For Oris, even the idea of going to a professional hair salon made her feel disloyal to her mother and grandmother. They had instilled a sense of personal duty to take care of her hair herself. They started seasoning her for the hair thing as soon as she could hold a brush. If *they could do it for themselves, so can I* was the refrain that repeated itself in her head.

The temperature of the dryer pulled her from her day-dreaming. The hot air blew against her temples and across the top of her ears. The hotter the temperature of the dryer, the quicker she would be done. She could stand the discomfort of much more heat than this dryer could dish out. This wasn't as bad as when she was a girl in her mother's kitchen, where she would sit for hours while her hair was tamed with a comb heated on the stove.

As her mom pulled her hair through the hot comb, she would scream out, "Ma, that hurts!" And her mother would reply, "If you'd sit still, it wouldn't hurt." The process was always the same. The wet hair, parted and twisted, segregated into squares, would be dried with the comb heated on the kitchen stove. She could hear the sizzle as the steam rose from the hair and curled around her mother's hand. The repetitive motion of the comb being pulled through the hair over and over, until it was dry and straight, was calming. She could hear her mother's voice as she announced "perfect" when the hair was done. No dryers or store-bought rollers for her when she was a little girl; Oris had watched and learned from her mother that strips of paper were the best material for wetting her kind of hair. The sound the paper rollers made as she turned in her sleep assured her that when she went to school no one would think her a poor, unkempt child.

Oris let her thoughts drift to the possibility of looking wild at the faculty party. What would the other faculty wives think? What would Russell think? She knew that Russell wouldn't hesitate to let her know what he thought. Pushing the hood of the old dryer off her head, she stood looking at the portraits of her family that hung in the abandoned room. She longed to ask the advice of the women whose pictures covered the peeling wall paper. The men, their bald heads shining as if anointed by heaven's only angels, appeared smug and satisfied. If she continued to use chemicals on her scalp, she might look like them someday. With each new application of chemicals and year of age, she was losing hair that did not grow back.

The women looked solid, dependable, and plain. They were

matronly martyrs serving their time on earth, their hair hidden under hats, waiting to ascend to their just reward. "A woman's hair is her crowning glory," she could hear her mother saying as she pulled, yanked, forcing every strand into a braid. It had been clear to eight-year-old Oris that grown-up women in her family kept their crowning glory to themselves. One great-aunt's hair was so severely pulled out of sight that she looked like someone had used a gray crayon to color in a scalp.

One exception did exist in her family. Oris' mother called her "Sunny, my play sister." Her portrait, taken when she was sixteen, hung on a wall of its own. Aunt Sunny smiled back at Oris. Her hair, parted in the middle, rushed in rippling currents down to her breast. It was never clear how she had become "play sister" or aunt. Church women whispered "hussy" as she walked down the aisle to take Communion on Sundays. They suggested that she cover her head in church. They didn't miss the smile that appeared on the preacher's face as he watched her approach him, kneel, and slowly push her tongue out to take the cracker he offered her. Oris' mother had slapped her hard once when she caught her in front of the mirror imitating Aunt Sunny's way of sticking out her tongue. The church women didn't miss the sound the preacher's wife made as he did his holy dance down the aisle of the church, urging his congregation to pray for forgiveness. After witnessing the Sunday drama, Oris' mother left the church mumbling how going to church without a hat was like saying good morning to the world without your clothes on.

Oris' visual tour of the room ended at the dresser that had belonged to Sunny. Oris' mother called it a silly piece of furniture bought for a vain woman. The family story was that Sunny had died combing her hair in front of the dresser's large, ornately carved mirror. As a young girl, Oris had spent hours watching her aunt at the mirror. Aunt Sunny died, willing the dresser to her.

"Oris, are you going to be in there all day?" Russell called to her. "What's for lunch?"

"Almost done," she yelled back. "This hair stuff has to stop," she said, talking to herself. "Sunny, help me?" Oris pleaded, staring into the mirror. She waited for an answer. "Sunny's not here. You have to help yourself." She sounded exactly like her mother. Propelled by forces she did not understand, Oris stood up suddenly, screaming, "ENOUGH! Enough!"

"Who are you talking to?" Russell wanted to know from the

bottom of the stairs.

Oris' hand reached into the sewing basket that sat on the floor. Her movements were decisive as she took the scissors out. As one hand pulled the plastic roller out from her scalp and the other held the scissors open, the blades refused to allow any impediments to their embrace. One blue plastic roller, with the damp graying hair still wrapped around it, bounced off her body like a ping pong ball. She heard Russell call to her as he started up the stairs. She didn't answer.

Staring into the mirror, Oris watched her hands, the left one wearing her wedding ring, race back and forth, cut the rollers from her head, then come to rest on her lap. Like the sea after a storm, she felt calm as she surveyed the aftermath. Varying lengths of hair like flattened snakes lay abandoned by the rollers on the floor. Hugging her scalp, some of the remaining hair curled into itself while the rest stretched upward as if shocked by a bolt of electricity. She pulled at the pieces near the front of her head. They sprang back like coiled wire, their resistance signaling life. She squeezed them between her fingers and tried to caress them into shape. The hair would not be pulled or cajoled into any style.

"Ooh," said Oris, feeling lightheaded as she stood peering into the mirror at a part of her blackness that had been suppressed all these years. She laughed with the beautiful black woman whose hair was frizzing up just a bit around the edge of her ears.

"O, how 'bout I take you out for a drink before the banquet?" Russell was saying as he came to a stop in the open door. His mouth opened. A revolution played on his face. Seconds passed. Oris stood ready.

"Damn, baby, what did you do to yourself?"

ELENA HARAP

MARYANNE WITHOUT MAKEUP
For Maryanne Crayton

her face the color of walnut
carved: planes, hollows, lines that speak—
her mother's face, a history made clear

her daily face
with tints of rose and lavender
cannot compare with this

this landscape endures
speaks knowledge: strong high cheekbones
     sadness: hollows in the cheeks
     purpose: clear set of mouth and chin
beauty beyond correction.

LI MIN MO

THE STORY OF MEILING

Excerpt from Wolfwoman, *a novel in progress*

China, 1800

An old fortune teller had predicted, "This one of your daughters is destined to run away; she cannot be tamed or bound, for she was marked by the spirit of the Wolfwoman, the half woman, half beast of the mountain." This divination had upset little Meiling's mother, and she worried about the future of her daughter. The mother wanted her daughter to marry someone well off; so, when Meiling was around seven, her mother started bending her toes backward and wrapping a long gauze tightly around her toes and feet.

"Little Meiling, I know this is going to hurt a lot, but swallow your tears, eat a little bitterness now, and some day your small lotus feet will earn you a rich husband. I should have started this when you were five, but you got sick that year," her mother said, bending the girl's toes backward and wrapping a long piece of gauze tightly over her feet. The little girl tried to wrestle her feet away, but her mother held them firm. Meiling thrashed her small arms in the air and screamed.

Later, admiring her careful work, the mother said with much affection, "Look at those pretty lotus feet, your future husband will adore you more." Meiling cried herself to sleep. The pain of the bound feet grew each day. Her mother was right about starting early, when the youngster was less likely to resist and fight back. Now little Meiling had to be subdued by three cousins and an aunt every night when her mother unwound the cloth around her bent toes for a short while, so the circulation of blood would not be cut short by the day binding; afterwards the mother wound the cloth back again for the night.

Each night the pain in her feet ripped through her whole body, and Meiling would wake up scared and confused. In the dark she gnawed at the gauze until it loosened. The next day her mother would resume the process.

On a full-moon night, three weeks after the foot binding began, Meiling ran away. She had loosened her gauze, this time with the help of a sharp flint she had found around the stove during the day. Her toes were sore, but the bones were not yet broken.

The hill country of Wei village was dotted with mud hummocks which looked like mounds or irregularities of the yellow earth. Its soil was the poorest in the region, dirt washed clean by the Wei river. The mineral-rich earth was most suitable as clay. There used to be a thriving pottery business in this desolate village, but that was a long time ago. In the distant north, a massive mountain range loomed, a watershed that divided the two great rivers, the Yellow River and the Yangtze River. To the north were the remains of a forest; to the west, hills and the beginning spread of a desert and a mountain range. The present small farming community had migrated here two generations ago to escape the flood of the Yellow River. The people of Wei used the long row of deserted mud kilns, located on a ledge in a high hill, for storage, but they ignored the old terracotta Earth Mother Goddess Temple nearby that had been erected by the potters who had fled the region long ago. The mud structure had fallen into disrepair, and only a large mud statue remained standing.

The dry hills seemed to stretch in all directions, touching the dark sky; Meiling didn't know where to go. The moon was full and bright. Strangely, it reminded her of the face of the broken mud statue. The red terracotta Earth Mother deity sat on a worn mud altar; her face was earth-red and round, with a half smile and a chipped-off nose. The statue had been there for a long time, but it was in such poor condition, no one went there with offerings or prayers any more. Children usually gathered there to play in the early evenings when they had finished their day's work.

Tonight, with the aid of the moon, like a pilgrim Meiling crawled to the ruins of the shrine and asked the goddess for protection. She knelt in front of the broken statue, sobbing and murmuring, "Protect me, Earth Mother Goddess, let me have my feet. I want to run, I want to jump." Pressing her palms together, she bowed and bowed. When she looked up at the earth statue without a nose, she thought the deity was smiling at her and had turned the bulk of its body. There, next to the statue was an opening; she probably hadn't noticed it before. Moving closer she slid her body into it and found a very cozy hideout, a small, round, underground mud cave lined with pieces of worn goat hide. They were probably the remains of sacrificial animals that had been offered to the goddess, or seating mats for shamans who had used the hole as their ritual winter retreat.

Once settled into the spot, Meiling felt protected. During the night, Meiling discovered that if she stretched her feet, she pushed some device that would shift the position of the statue and close the hole. Later she could push again, crawl out safely, and venture home. First she would hide in the pig pen and wait for the sound of her family to quiet down, the fire to go out; then she tiptoed into the kitchen to scrounge for food.

Meiling's family was perplexed by her disappearance. They sent a small search party to look for her, but no one found her. After two weeks the family thought she must have been snatched by the wolves that roamed in the hills at night, sighted occasionally by country folks traveling across the border.

Three weeks passed. Meiling's mother had given up hope that her daughter was still alive. The little girl had grown accustomed to living in the pit in the day and searching for food at night, until one night her head burned with fever and she was too weak to crawl out. The following night she was so sick she didn't even open her eyes.

A small girl, playing around the old ruins the next day, digging around the base of the Earth Mother statue for what she thought was a small coin stuck between the cracks, heard a human voice under the statue, rushed home, and told everyone that she had overheard the voice of her lost cousin Meiling. Most of the members of the family told her she was making up a story, and some told her to stop telling lies. But one of Meiling's older cousins took an interest and decided to investigate. The young man went to the abandoned sacred site and poked around the base of the earth statue. He, too heard a cry, "Ma, ma," under it. Later, half a dozen men were assembled and with great effort managed to hoist the statue and free the sick little Meiling.

Everyone in the village rejoiced and hailed Meiling as someone who had performed a miracle, moving an earth statue to give herself shelter for three weeks. She was also hailed as the sacred child of the Earth Mother Goddess, a child endowed with luck and magic. Her mother stopped binding her feet. All goddesses had big feet.

Meiling's fame spread to other villages. Matchmakers came and begged to match her to rich landlords. The family wanted to wait until their girl turned thirteen or fourteen. But on her eleventh birthday, a storm-flood came and everything the family possessed was destroyed or washed away. A well-known landlord, Old Man Liu, offered assistance in the form of high interest loans and farming supplies in exchange for the sacred girl as his concubine. He already had three wives. Two of the three had no children and the first one bore only daughters. A girl who had directly received protection from the Earth Goddess was prized as someone who would bring good luck to the family. Working on commission, the matchmaker used her inventiveness and persuaded the Liu family that the girl was also endowed with magic and that she would bring prosperity and great wealth.

For a traditional wedding, her father had to borrow money to give a banquet for seventy guests and relatives. All Meiling remembered was the loud, piercing wedding music her uncle Lung was blowing with his double-reed pipe and everyone slurping down large bowls of noodles with slices of pork fat and toasting with cups of warm *kaoliang* wine. She didn't want to eat or drink, she just wanted the festivity to end and the darkness of the night to swallow her. She was choking on her sobs. Her sorrow and fear seemed to haunt her like the cries of the pipe music. Amidst shouts, the Liu family members raised her up onto a red sedan chair that would carry her to her future home.

There was a good distance to travel, and she listened to the fading pipe music until it was just a murmur, a rustling of wind. The sedan chair bobbed up and down, and she heard the porters' heaving breaths. She took off the red satin cloth on her head and pulled the sedan chair's curtain aside to peek out. The moon was new and the night air fresh. She felt alone, scared, and hopelessly weak. Squeezing the scarlet head cloth in her hands, she felt a chill, an uncontrollable shaking. An intense pain started in her stomach, then traveled down her legs, until her whole lower body was stiff and paralyzed.

Liu's wives and servants came out to help carry the new bride inside the brightly lit house. They forced warm tea down her throat, then rubbed tiger-bone wine all over her legs. They massaged her until her body was warm, and then they left her alone in the bedchamber. Meiling heard the three wives chatter on their way out of the room.

"That poor thing, she is just a skinny child. Is she the girl from Wei village?"

"Look, we were all like that when we were first brought into this house."

"Well, I was fourteen and I was not as scared as her."

"I was half drunk and remembered nothing of the first night."

Meiling sat up in the canopy bed with its red silk spread and red silk pillows embroidered with dragons and phoenixes. All the red, that color of luck, only kindled her fear and anguish. Her legs seemed warmed up a little, but her stomach still felt queasy and crampy. She curled her small body, hugging her knees to her stomach, and dozed off in that position, until a loud laugh right next to her shook her out of her rest. It was dark in the room and she could only smell the hot breath of Old Man Liu, fetid with rice wine and cigars. He grabbed her like a cat capturing a mouse. He tore her red shirt off and her red pants, ripping them as if he were skinning an animal. She felt and heard the satin cloth being torn as if it were her flesh. Refusing to uncurl herself, she tried to fight off his advance. The old man was high on rice wine and took her defense as a game. Roaring with laughter, he picked up the helpless girl. Pushing her face into the pillow, he tried to penetrate her from the back, but couldn't. Eventually he overpowered her. Later he took her shredded red pants and tied her, one hand on each bed post. She tried to bite him whenever he put his hand over her mouth. Before he left her alone, he stuffed her mouth with cloth and tied her legs together.

"You stupid girl, you don't want to submit to your master. You're getting what you deserve," Liu hollered, and then he thought about what he had heard, that this Meiling girl was supposed to be a good luck charm and had power. But she hadn't demonstrated her magic. "Tricks and lies, stories that matchmakers boast!!" the old man exclaimed. He staggered out of the room, muttering, "We'll see what kind of magic girl you are. I want to see something . . . ."

The following day, one of the wives came to visit Meiling and tried to talk some sense into her. While two servants untied the girl, washed her with hot washcloths, and changed the sheet, the first wife sat beside the ornately carved, round teak table.

"Call me Ahmei," she introduced herself. The woman was decked out with jewels, her face skillfully made up. Sipping hot tea, the lovely woman consoled Meiling. "You're a woman, and a poor one, too. But your fate is not so bitter yet. You have been married to a wealthy man. Liu is rich and powerful. You have not just a roof over your head, but a mansion with rooms, courtyards, gardens, and servants at your command; not just three meals every day, but any fancy food you would like to taste, pretty silk clothes to wear, and outings to festivals and shows. If you bear the old man a son, he will reward you with jewels and other gifts.

"What's wrong with you, girl?" the head-wife questioned, noticing the angry and pensive expression on Meiling's face.

She sounded like a kind woman, thought Meiling. "I don't know why I refused to give in. I really don't understand why my body just got stiff and fearful whenever the old man touched me," the young girl confessed.

"Try to think about the brighter side of things. We are women and this is our fate, to be married and bear children." As the head wife, she certainly sounded more benevolent than competitive, mean, or envious of new and younger wives' position.

However, Meiling's fate was destined to be bitter and unlucky. She refused to give in to the old man. Each night she fought with him, she bit him, scratched him when he let her loose. One night he bought a half dozen huge, black bugs and let them crawl on her naked chest. The bugs scared her in the beginning, but eventually they tickled her everywhere and caused her whole body to convulse. Old Man Liu took delight in her fear and her helpless, shaking body. There was the traditional belief that if a male held back ejaculation, his Yang energy would be preserved. The old man's own sexual excitement was extended somehow by his torture of poor Meiling for hours. Later, exhausted from his own exertion, he collapsed on her, crushed her with his weight while ejaculating and later urinating all over her stiff and sore body.

During the day, Meiling was tired and disoriented. Everything around her turned murky as if shrouded by dark clouds. Liu's three wives spent most of their time playing mah-jong and cards, dressing up for afternoon shows in the garden, entertaining visitors, supervising servants in food preparation, shopping, cleaning, gardening, and caring for children and elders. Meiling usually sat in her bedroom after servants had helped wash and dress her.

The head-wife of the Lius came to see her every day, consoling her and encouraging her to eat and go out to enjoy the garden. "If you sit inside all the time, you'll turn crazy. You'll get used to being a woman, a wife, and forget about your childhood," she said to Meiling. The girl bride, unmoved by the woman's kind words, stared blankly into space. "Tomorrow you'll have to join us for a wonderful puppet show in the open courtyard. You'll love this troupe; they are going to do the 'Journey to the West.'" Just before she stepped out of the room, she said, "Meiling mei-mei, it's for your own good to cheer up a little. Old Man Liu will soon get bored with you and he will look for others to play with. And when that day comes, you'll be able to really enjoy your life."

When the kind first wife left, Meiling put her head on the teakwood table and sobbed. She had no words for her pain, or ways to describe the assaults she had to endure at night. She thought back to her home up in the hill country, back to that morning when the storm had come with its unrelenting torrents and avenging wind that tore up everything in sight. Eventually, her whole village had been submerged. Some neighbors witnessed the oncoming storm in an adjacent town and rushed back to warn everyone, but the poor farming folk had no place to run to. The only structures that were up high, still dry, were the old kilns located not far from Meiling's family compound. So the whole family of six, including three pigs, six hens, and two roosters, huddled together, taking refuge in several terracotta kilns that were shaped like small caves.

Watching the onslaught of water and wind, the family was utterly helpless. Their mud cottage was destroyed; so were their pigpens and their storehouse of grain. Her mother covered her face with her hands, muttering a cry that sounded like the gurgles and groans of wounded creatures. "Old heaven has no eyes, old heaven has no eyes, aiiii, aiiii, aiiii!" She wailed for many hours, while Meiling's father was stricken dumb by the disaster.

Two days later, a foot of muddy sludge covered everything. For weeks her family tried to salvage what was still usable, scraping mud off kitchen utensils, farm tools, bamboo furniture, and scrap wood from the wreckage. The storm and the flood had diminished their hope and completely wiped out their fall harvest and their storehouse for the coming winter. If it hadn't been for this disaster, Meiling knew her family wouldn't have consented to match her with Old Man Liu from a distant village near the Hsiang Mountain. The rich landlord was known for his hideous cruelty towards his wives and servants. Behind his back, the people in Meiling's village had labeled him a monster, *Liulokue-Niokuema*. She had heard stories about these monsters, *Niokuema*, or Bull-demon-horses, and how they devoured humans, especially young children, in order to achieve immortality. Meiling had given a lot of thought to running away from Liu's household, but she had not been left alone since she arrived. There was always a servant or two in her room.

The sounds of the loud banging of brass cymbals and small gongs, and the clapping of bamboo-sticks brought her back to her present world. She caught a glimpse of a troupe of puppeteers marching by her window. The sound of entertainment and celebration only heightened the pain and anguish in her body and heart. Luckily, that night the Old Man Liu went to a party and stayed over at his guest's house, and Meiling had her first night of peace since her wedding five days before. The next day, Ahmei, the first wife, came to her room and woke her.

"Meiling, it's past noon. And the puppet show is going to perform again in the east courtyard." The first wife stroked the girl's cheeks with one hand and said, "You remind me of my daughter whom I lost last year. She had a fearless, handsome expression, like yours; especially those clear and gorgeous eyes of yours, they are just like my daughter's were." Ahmei took out her silk handkerchief and wiped away the tears that rolled down her cheeks.

"What happened to her?" Meiling was shocked by her own blunt and straightforward question.

"Aiii, my heart, my heart," the wife started to sob uncontrollably. The servants around her escorted her out while one of them gently rubbed her back. The girl overheard one of them whisper to the wife, "You've got to forget that incident. It is not good for your health to think about your daughter."

Meiling sat in the room throughout the day, until the servants brought her supper and hot water in a basin to wash her hands. Like a puppet, the young bride let them manipulate her body; she even let them spoon-feed her as if she were an invalid. Right after the servants had finished with her, they heard an unexpected noise from the outside corridors. A group of servants and wives rushed by, and one of Meiling's servants went out to inquire. She was back shortly and announced to the other two servants and to Meiling, the fourth wife of Old Man Liu, "Master Liu has 'walked-away' on his way back from the party." The servant who delivered the news arched her eyebrows, twisted her mouth, and burst into a sob that sounded fake. The other two servants also began faking grief, chanting "Aieeee, aieeee," while pounding their foreheads with their fists. Meiling thought they looked rather comical. When they finished throwing a theatrical fit, one of them cried out, "Hurry up, let's rush out to the courtyard! There's a lot of work to do." Everyone left the room, leaving Meiling sitting there all by herself. There was no reaction; she didn't know what to think, now that her tormentor had gone.

The following week was exceptionally busy for everyone in

the Liu household. The new bride was temporarily forgotten. A rich man's funeral was more elaborate than his wedding ceremony. A big band was hired, and a group of professional mourners were paid to lead the procession. The young girl had never attended a big funeral of a rich man before. The servants came and dressed Meiling in white burlap.

The march was headed by reed pipers, followed by the wailing paid mourners all covered from head to toe with white burlap gowns. Finally the rich relatives came, carried on sedan chairs, the coffin and its bearers, servants, and porters hauling food and provisions on foot. They marched through the village and headed to the mountain. The days were getting cold, and the wind threatened to blow their mourning hoods off their heads, yet everyone kept pace and followed the blaring reed pipers. They had walked for five or six miles when they stopped for a break. The servants set out some soup, steamed bread and tea. Some people sat on the ground and looked up at the sky.

The rumor had started: the sacred Earth Goddess girl was supposed to bring fortune and good luck to Liu's household, but she had brought on the death of their master and bad luck for the entire family. "The Wu family tricked us," one relative complained, sipping wine from a small earthen flask.

"I really doubted that puny little girl had any magical power," remarked another man, stuffing a handful of peanuts into his mouth. The talk about the good-luck girl Meiling turning into a bad-luck girl continued to spread.

"She should perform a miracle for us: bring back master Liu," one wife suggested.

"That's it. If she was able to cause the Earth Goddess to move, she can bring life back from death," remarked another relative. It didn't take long for the crowd of mourners to rally behind that idea. One of the Taoist priests who was hired to perform the funeral rite said, "We should leave this girl here, next to Master Liu's grave. And give her two servants and enough provisions for seven days." Everyone thought that was a great idea; seven days would be long enough for the new bride to perform a magical act if she was the sacred Earth Goddess girl.

The crowd was ready to resume their climb after packing up their provisions. The mourners felt rested, energized, but also hopeful that the funeral march might turn into a resurrection march. All the way up the steep hill, people cried and cheered. Meiling was the exception; she was dumbfounded and had difficulty in lifting her legs and keeping pace with the others. Finally she could no longer climb, but collapsed on the ground. The Taoist priest came over, mumbled some words over her, and waved his horsehair whisk in front of her face. Someone squirted wine into her mouth, another picked her up and carried her up the hill.

When they arrived at the Liu family burial plot, six men started to dig. The Taoist priest chanted in monotone over the coffin and then over Meiling, who was sitting on the ground with her head in her hands. There was incense smoke in the air, folded spirit paper ingots burning in large trays, red candles lit, and small cups of wine poured around the grave site. Little dishes of food were set out. All these were for the ghosts and spirits. Small pots of flowers were also planted in front of the gravestone. Paper gowns, paper houses, and big bundles of fake money were loaded into a large, colorful paper-boat. All the relatives bowed and wailed. At the end of the funeral rite, the Taoist priest set all the paper goods on fire.

The crowd took off just before dusk. The priest ordered two servants to take care of the fourth wife and assist her in any rituals she might perform over the grave. If Meiling couldn't call on the Earth Goddess to aid her as she had done once before, she would be severely punished. The servant boys were scared of the mountain and graves scattered all over the hills. They eyed each other and then the child bride, sacred Earth Goddess girl.

"Hey, why don't you start to work, perform the miracle. We don't want to stay here for seven days," the taller boy yelled.

"There must be wild beasts, ghosts, and demons roaming in this part of the country," proclaimed the other.

Meiling didn't feel like talking or responding to them. She was not afraid of the hills or the darkness descending. What to do about the dead old man? She had no desire to see him alive again. There were days when she had actually prayed for him to die. Maybe her prayers were granted. Suddenly she felt good and cheerful again; tonight she would not have to submit to the old man's torment. When night enveloped the whole region, all three children fell asleep, exhausted from their day's climb and mourning.

They had no strange encounters on their first night next to Old Man Liu's grave. The second day the three cooperated in hoisting up a makeshift canopy for their night's lodging. Meiling was in good spirits. Together they went around the hills and gathered wild greens to supplement the dry food they were given by the Lius. One boy started a fire with kindling he had gathered, and the other found dried animal dung to add to it. They looked like peasant boys, thought the girl.

"How old are you two?" she asked.

"Thirteen, and my brother is ten," answered the taller one.

"Which village are you from?"

"Hsia village, not far from here," answered the younger.

"Did you really cause the Mother Earth deity to move?" the older boy asked.

She nodded and said, "I wasn't sure what really happened. I was seven then."

"I don't want to stay here for a week. Why don't you try to bring master Liu back to life now?" said the younger boy.

The girl didn't respond; she sat on the ground and studied Old Man Liu's grave. The candles were still burning, the flowers were blooming, the little offering saucers were emptied, no more incense burned, and the fresh mound of earth was soft. She stared into the fire the boys had made and said in a passive tone,

"I am glad that Old Man Liu is dead. He is not going to come back to life; I am praying hard for that." The girl closed her eyes and joined her palms together and prayed. The two boys were astonished. They eyed each other and the younger one muttered, "This girl is crazy. We can't go home until she brings the old man back from death." The older boy went over to Meiling and shouted, "You got to bring the old man back to life. The priest told you to perform some rituals. Are you going to disobey his command?"

The girl jumped up and shouted back, "Hey, are you out of your mind? Old Man Liu is a monster and he is better dead." She felt as if she were going to strike the boy, but he looked so pitiful and sad, she held herself back. "You two are free to go back to your village. You don't have to stay with me."

The two boys started to sob. "We don't have a home any more," the tall boy revealed, "our family was destroyed by the storm. Our parents were crushed to death when the roof collapsed on them. We were sold to Liu's house by our uncle."

Meiling was sympathetic. "My family home was destroyed by the storm, too. There is no use to cry all night. Let's cook some food. Aren't you hungry?" The two immediately responded, "Oh, yes, we are very hungry." They wiped the tears with their sleeves and rose up to help with food preparation. She told one of them to fetch water a mile down the hill from a small stream that they had spotted while climbing the mountain the day before. She and the other boy went to collect more fuel. They had been given a rich variety of food—fresh wheat noodles, salted meats, mushrooms, seaweed, soy sauce, peanut oil, sausages, and a large basket of buns.

The three youngsters didn't exchange any words while they ate. Later the girl confessed, "Listen to me, I am not trying to make life harder than it already is. If I had any magic power, I would wish to be home with my family. I really miss my grandmother, my uncle Lung, my three sisters and two brothers." The girl started to cry, but continued, "I have prayed for magic power ever since the day I was betrothed to Old Man Liu, but to no avail. You see, I am no different from you two; I am a peasant girl from the Wei village, not far from Hsia, and . . ." She noticed the boys were scratching their heads and shuffling their straw sandals on the ground.

"Don't you believe me? I'm telling the truth," Meiling said.

The boys listened, kept their thoughts to themselves about the young widow of Liu, and continued to stare at her as if she were a total stranger. Getting no response from the two, Meiling got up and started to prepare her bedding for the night. The older boy rose up slowly, motioned to his brother to follow him, and tramped into the woods. When the two came out, they tied the food in burlap, making a half dozen small bundles, and hoisted them up on the branches of a nearby tree so the mice and other animals would not be able to get to them.

The girl fell asleep the moment it got dark. She was not aware of how tired and stressed she had been for the past week. Now she felt relieved, free to rest and dream; she had no plans for tomorrow or the future. In her dark sleep she was floating on a raft all by herself, trying to reach Putoe Island, the island inhabited by immortals. Suddenly a three-headed serpent rose out of the sea and opened its huge mouth. Sharp fangs descended to engulf her. She tried to fight back with her long oars, but the sea monster was too powerful; in one gulp it had devoured her whole, raft and all. The dark cavity inside the monster became her home.

Sounds of mice woke her. Even in the dark she could tell they were everywhere and could sense them crawling around her legs. Immediately she bolted upright and sent the mice scurrying. When dawn came, Meiling noticed something had changed overnight; the canopy above her had disappeared and the two servant boys were not sleeping nearby. When she looked around she discovered that the six bundles of food suspended from the branches of the tree were no longer there. Numerous baskets of utensils, pots, and dishes were gone, too. Even the offering dishes in front of the gravestone were taken. The boys had stolen everything and run away during the night.

For a long time Meiling just sat on the ground, staring into the hills that were dotted with gravestones. When she came to her senses, she started climbing down the mountain. She vaguely remembered how to get back to Liu's village, but she was afraid the people there would punish her for not having performed a miracle. She was not sure of the way to the Hsia village until she found a track made by those boys, dragging their loot down the hill. At the foot of the mountain, the track from the two boys changed; the ground was mushy, and it seemed to her that there were many people's footprints. One set was heading back to the mountain, another was trailing off into the woods, and one was leading down the hill. Meiling was completely puzzled by all these footprints. Which ones should she follow? Meiling, lost in the mountain, decided to play a children's game to determine her direction. She spun to the count of one hundred and the minute she stopped her count, pointed her right hand straight ahead. That was her route. Had she taken a roundabout way out of the mountain or had she traveled deeper into it? When the sun started to slide to the other side of the horizon, she had also climbed several hills, deeper into the woods. There were no more gravestones, just tall grass and flowers. A lovely scent of wild herbs wafted in the air, and in the distance there was a thin thread of smoke. It might be a cooking fire, thought the girl, so she hiked towards it. The smoke actually was quite faraway, but Meiling was determined to get there, for she was terrified of the possibility of staying alone overnight in the woods. Parts of the rocky path were covered with wild thorny vines. Luckily her body was covered with several layers of a burlap mourning gown and only her feet were bruised by the hike.

By nightfall she had come closer to the place of the smoke. From a short distance away she saw a small blaze, but there was no one tending it. Mustering some courage, the girl stalked closer to it, took off her mourning gown, and sat down next to the fire to warm herself. Suddenly a furry beast sprang up before her eyes, arched its sharp claws in front of its dark face and howled; it seemed to have leapt out from nowhere. The girl screamed and fell backwards.

When she opened her eyes, she was faced with an old woman who had more wrinkles on her dark face than any great-grandmother she had ever encountered back in her village. The woman's whole body, from her head to her toes, was covered with dark animal fur. The young girl was scared of her and thought this must have been the wolfwoman she had heard about. The woman didn't speak or make any other sound; she dug into the edge of the fire, pulled out several large roasted sweet potatoes, gave one to the girl, and motioned her to eat. A minute ago Meiling had craved something to eat, but now she was dominated by fear.

The way animals would wait—you don't make a move; I don't make a move—the two of them just sat opposite each other across the fire. Not a body twitch or a sound passed between them. The old one looked as if she were dozing off while sitting upright. The young girl stared into the fire and felt like a captive. Meiling thought if this was the wolfwoman, she would rip the girl apart and eat her for dinner. Suddenly the old woman picked up the roasted sweet potatoes by her feet and ate. After she had devoured four of them, she pulled out a little gourd tied to a belt around her waist and drank from it. From the dark ground she grabbed something that looked like a huge dried ginseng and gnawed at it noisily for a long while. When she had finished her evening eating, she lay down and fell asleep.

Meiling waited until it seemed to her that the old one was no longer twitching and shifting; she then turned and started to crawl out of the fire circle. It was pitch dark all around her. All she could make out was a swarm of fireflies above some tall grass. The sky was gray, the moon was hiding, revealing just a little light. It was difficult for her to know which way to crawl or what path to take to get herself out. Suddenly there was the wolfwoman, less than three feet directly across from her, staring at Meiling with her large, bright eyes. How come she didn't even hear the woman move? How had she suddenly landed in front of her? Meiling rubbed her eyes with disbelief. When she looked again, the old woman wasn't there anymore. She moved ahead on all fours with great caution; every ten feet or so the wolfwoman would appear in front of her, staring at her but without advancing toward her. Then, just as before, she would disappear, leaving the girl frightened and disoriented.

It was like playing the children's game of "You Are IT." Everyone would make a move behind the child who was IT, who had her back turned from the crowd, eyes covered, while calling out, "One, two, three, look out!" When IT turned around, opened her eyes and shouted "You are IT," every player had to stop moving. If IT caught anyone moving, that player would become IT. Tonight the wolfwoman was playing "You Are IT" with Meiling. To the girl, the game was life and death, to the old woman it was just a night catching game. As the night wore on, the girl was finally defeated; she had become the eternal IT. She collapsed on the ground, tugged herself into a heap, and sobbed. The old one left her alone. In the dark she felt someone throw a furry cover on top of her. Soon she fell asleep.

In the morning the girl woke and noticed the entire mountain was enveloped in dense fog. Smoke or air currents like silver gauze moved in a haunting manner in the distance. Meiling had never been this deep in the woods before. Everything was changing before her eyes, yet she could not distinguish what it was. She felt strange, but at the same time not as afraid as the night before. She rose and stretched her stiff muscles, then walked toward the small fire. The old woman with the fur was sitting in front of it, turning some sticks that had small pieces of meat stuck on them. The girl was famished. When the old one handed her a stick of meat she took it, sat down next to the fire, and ate.

"Don't be afraid of me, child," the old one said in a deep and kind voice, "drink a little tea." She handed Meiling a small gourd. The girl took a small draft of the liquid; it was a bitter brew, worse than the medicine her mother used to feed her when she was ill. It made her choke and shake.

"You'll get used to this stuff. It's really good for you; it'll make your liver and kidney strong," the old one said, and took a drink herself.

"Why are you traveling all alone in this part of the mountain?" she asked.

Meiling hesitated to answer, but after a long pause she recounted, "I was left next to my husband's grave two days ago. The Lius wanted me to perform a miracle in bringing the old man back to life."

"You are only a child and you've already gone through a lot, I see. People always wish for miracles. This is not a safe place. There are bandits, grave robbers, escaped criminals, and all sorts of troublemaking people hiding in this mountain. And to tell you the truth, men are more dangerous and cruel than the animals who live here."

"I have no place to go. If I go back to the village, the Lius will punish me. And if I run back to my mother's house, they probably will find me." The girl started to cry.

"Come, come, don't you get me sad, child. Now that you have bumped into me, you'll stay with me and I'll teach you how to get along in this unruly place," the old one comforted her. "I have to head back up in the mountain. The cold days are coming and I have to prepare my winter home. Here, eat some more. We have a long hike ahead of us and weeks of hard work." Her kind voice and gentle manner won the trust of the young girl.

Hidden in a thorny briar patch, the old woman had stored a large bag of ginseng. Several huge bags of medicine were hung on a tree, and there were countless strings of dried fruits and meats strung through strands of twine.

"You see, my child, I usually spend a great deal of time during the early fall in this wild valley, digging ginseng, gathering medicine, drying wild vegetables and fruits. That's the way to get through the harsh days of winter. Well, occasionally I do go out to set my traps for some meat."

"How are you going to carry these things up the hills?" asked the girl as she helped tie everything into bundles.

"Oh, it's easy," replied the old one, balancing a huge burlap bag on her back and a large bag on top of her head. "You only have to strap those strings of dried meat and fruits over your shoulder and follow me."

The girl had always considered herself a good climber, for ever since she was young she had loved to climb trees and race the hills with the boys of her village. But she was no match for the old woman, who was swift and agile despite the tremendous load on her back. The path the old one took was completely hidden by the fog; it was really hard to stay close behind her. It was like climbing blindfolded. Meiling had to trust her instinct and her sense of smell. Luckily the old one's bundle emitted a mixture of strong odors of fresh ginseng, moza, fennel, angelica root, wild onion. Led by her nose, the girl scaled some of the roughest steps of jagged granite. The straps that held the food bundles clung on her shoulders and bit, chafed, and bruised her. Several times Meiling had to stop to catch a breath or two. The old one kept going for hours, until they reached a flat boulder.

"This is Turtle Rock," said the old woman as she lifted her bundles off her back. Panting for breath, the girl collapsed on the rock.

"This is too hard. I don't think I'll be able to make it to the top," she said.

"My child, rest a little and drink a little tea. I'll rub your legs with this stuff and then you'll be able to make it." This time the girl took a big swig of that bitterest brew from the gourd, and once it traveled down her throat it made her feel refreshed. Next the old woman rubbed some smelly balm on her bare legs, which made them feel like they were on fire.

"Ouch, that stuff burnt me."

"Be patient, my child. It soon will relieve tension and soreness." And within a short time her muscles did feel better. "Here, chew on this ma huang stem; it will help you breathe while we ascend." The old woman put some strange, bittersweet tasting herb into her mouth. They resumed their climb and hours later they reached a shallow cave next to a huge boulder. "Here's our resting place for the night. Tomorrow we'll get up to my home."

The fog had lifted; a clear blue sky. Meiling noticed birds flying across the low-lying bushes. She looked around and could see far into the distant valley. The stony side might be the hill of graves. Rows of mud hummocks—that might be near the Lius.' Those strange-looking mounds, maybe they were the terracotta kilns around her own village. It was hard to tell. She was homesick and playing guessing games in her head. For the most part, the view was dominated by shades of green and the brown, yellow, gray sod, rough texture of boulders and stones.

"Here, you take that side. It's wider and has better bedding," called the old woman. The girl turned and noticed that not too far from where she was standing several layers of old woven straw matting covered the rough stone. The space was narrow and long. The old woman piled her stuff on the outer edge and lay down facing the stone wall. Meiling followed her example and soon fell asleep. In the middle of the night she was woken by strange crying, howling sounds. It was pitch black and she couldn't see anything. The old one spoke. "My child, those were cries of monkey. Do not be afraid." But the girl couldn't sleep any more. The mournful sound had made her sad and scared. She wished to be home with her family. Just before dawn the girl finally fell asleep.

Bird songs and the sun warming her face woke her. The old one was already up and working on some tangled rope.

"I am going to climb up this cliff, then pull the stuff up, and afterwards I will pull you up." Effortlessly the old woman scaled the cliff with one end of the long rope tied around her waist and the other end fastened to her bundles. When she got to the top, she started to pull her things up. Later she threw the rope to the girl and asked her to tie it around her waist.

"Now, grab on tight to the rope with both your hands." That was how she got to the wolfwoman's house, a cave on top of a tall cliff, its opening facing the south.

The old one never mentioned how she ended up in the wild and how come she had no family. The young girl thought, *Wolfwoman must have had to run away from her village when she was being treated cruelly. It probably was too painful for her to talk about it.* Where and how did she acquire the wolf skin? How did she get so strong? How long had she lived on the mountain by herself? Meiling was very curious, but it would have been rude for her to pry into the past of an elder.

One day, right after practicing how to leap and climb, she thought maybe this was the right time to ask; after all, she had been a helpful disciple and had been obedient for months.

"How did you end up being covered with a wolf coat, Granny?"

"Oh that was a story from long ago," the old one said, but didn't give her any answers.

Aura Luz Sanchez

CELINE

Notes: *Panas*, breadfruit; *yautia*, a root vegetable; *budins*, puddings, often bread pudding; *Hay Dios mio*, Oh, my God; *tontos*, jerks, dummies; *pendejos*, sexual putdown, a slang term; *'staran locas*, are you crazy.

Tough, sassy and holy Celine
flying up from the island
through a storm in '44, the four-prop plane
full of fear-stricken migrants,
their insides whipped up
as they rollercoasted
over heartstopping drops,
native fruit, slipped by US Customs,
spilling out of their brown shopping bags—
panas, yautias, budins from Aguada.

They clapped wildly that night
as they rumbled and tumbled into La Guardia.
Celine catapulted into our lives
with her *Hay Dios mio's*
her baby Evelina
and her overstuffed cardboard valise.

Celine, seductive Celine:
a gentleman of means
had left her with a white-skinned child.
"Just like an American!"
her relatives oohed;
a baby Olympian
set apart from her earth-colored cousins.

Celine, fiery Celine:
a misnomer,
nothing cold or lunar about her,
an Apollonian divinity,

disdainful of men who were *tontos, pendejos.*
Disbelief reflected
in her mischief brown eyes
at the thought of settling down.
"Marriage? Not for me—'*staran locas!*"
she'd click with her castanet tongue.

On second-hand shopping sprees
with her broken English and fluent street smarts
she'd finagle bargains from the vendors in La Marketa,
would kibbitz with the best
on the Lower East Side.

Undaunted by the home relief worker
with her sprung visits engineered
to catch the disallowed man
or the hand-me-down TV
under the chenille-faded spread,
"Me no speak eengleesh," Celine would mock
this overseer of the poor.

Celine, celestial Celine:
a super nova
spending her energy
on stormy affairs
and cold-water flats.
Then one summer day, the fatal eclipse.
A window gave way; her child lost her life.
Celine, trapped in a scream,
counterpoint to the creak of her rocker—
an abstraction in time with nowhere to go,
she rocks to and fro.

Celine, leaden Celine:
slow, purposeless years brought her
to the house of the Lord,
a Pentecostal rebirth;
her lights re-ignited.
Celine, radiant Celine.

Elena Harap

AUNT DEVRA SPEAKS

Note: *Samovar*, a Russian urn for making tea.

Yes, Morelli was my lover—why make a fuss?
I worked for his company forty years,
kept the books; right through the Depression and the War
we worked together. He was a wonderful guy, generous,
ran a good business, had a nice family. And for me
things weren't easy after Mama died.
Papa married a woman we children couldn't bear to live with
so we took a place in the Bronx, three brothers,
my little sister Rachel and me. Those younger ones were smart,
you know; Manny ended up at Harvard,
Rachel went to Antioch.
I had boyfriends. There was a Russian fellow
but he went off to the war, we lost touch.

Then I got the job at Morelli's. He used to send me flowers;
to him I was beautiful, I guess. I didn't dress
fancy, I had nice things; but he saw something more.
I never said anything, never troubled the family.
And I was a sister to my brothers' wives.
Only to Cousin Sara I confided
and she kept her silence.

Over the years I stayed in touch with everyone.
It was my pleasure, giving parties at my apartment in Queens
when the nieces and nephews came to town.
We'd all get together for dinner and talk about
which one looked like Papa or like Mama.

Look, Morelli was Catholic, he couldn't divorce;
besides, I would never destroy a family.
What's to tell you, really? Trips on the Hudson Day Line,
sitting on the deck to smoke and look up and down the river
(Rachel was always after me about my pack-a-day Lucky Strikes
but Morelli, with his cigars, it didn't bother him)—sometimes

we took a weekend. I'm not sorry.
I think maybe my married sisters never knew
what independence felt like: my place, my own linen,
my brass samovar; and I took trips on my own, too.

When Morelli died he remembered me in his will.
He left me half the shop building. I bought a winter home
in Florida; that's where my story ends.
Morelli had been gone for many years. I was tired
and had this problem in my inner ear, dizzy all the time, nothing
seemed to help it. I was ready to go.

A business man and a bookkeeper, that's what we were,
both short, and dark—me from Yanaf, him from Lipari.
I stopped dyeing my hair after he passed away. I left his
picture in my apartment along with all the family snapshots
and in a sealed envelope some pressed flowers
from a bouquet he picked for me. Morelli was always there,
in my life, my bed. I wanted you to know.

LI MIN MO

THE UNDERWORLD GODDESS OF P.S. 65

Thirty years later I still remember her
nasal "hum," the way she held anguish
between her brows.

Almost every morning she comes
in late, spreading her cheap cologne;
in her high-heeled gold slippers
she sashays to the third row from
the front. Her dyed-blond curls still
in rollers, face pale without makeup,
only black mascara, making the girls in
the eighth grade homeroom glance at her
sideways, the boys hold their breath,
stare at the blackboard while the whore
of Mott Street slides into her seat.
Her white leggings show off her buttocks,
a beige raincoat, unbuttoned, reveals
a red tank top that embraces her perfect,
full bosom, her painted red fingernails
spread like a spider web upon the
scratchy school desk, all carved up by
those punks who were bored with school
or felt doomed by their initials. *Napoleon,*
Alfonso, Juan, Francisco, became chiseled
vengeance, no different from the way she
feels, a misfit who becomes in just a few
minutes our heat of the day, our unrealized
fantasy, our underworld-goddess.

We want to inhale her whole, feel her
thighs rub against our faces, squeeze
her breasts, let her buttocks wiggle
on our laps, draw our tongues across
her belly, we want to suffocate
her with our desires, we want
to set her on fire . . .

One late night, walking down Mott Street,
I see her arguing with two cops; her green
eyes framed by fake eyelashes grow angry
with repeated mouthing of profanity.
They cuff her, shove her into the cruiser
. . . the siren calls are still ringing in my ears
as I descend into the subway. Where is
Persephone? Imagine Demeter's grief—
she'll roam across the land, perpetuate
winter on earth until her daughter is found.

Lord of the underworld traps her in
Bowery, where booze, tobacco smoke, violent
ways of penises, asses, semen, desperate
hands, insatiable hunger enslave her; she
swallows one pomegranate seed.

Aura Luz Sanchez

ANA Y COLO

Note: *Guayabera*, the pleated cotton shirt commonly worn by
men in Puerto Rico; *merengue*, Puerto Rican popular dance.

The camera captured the incongruity
trapping him in the space/time of
Brooklyn, 1963.

Wearing his *guayabera* with its vertical pleats,
his white hair parted
like a walrus' moustache,
he stands erect against the green walls
accented with splotches of pink
from my father's old shaving brush,
next to the liquor store calendar
of a New England snowy countryside.
My grandfather, Colo,
had followed my grandmother, Ana,
to New York six months before she died.

Ana was losing her mind,
turning deaf, going blind.
The clarity of a world caressed by sunlight
had crowded up
with graying blurs of spirits and shadows
whispering alarming untruths
in her idling ears,
inciting her repeated pleas
to deities and saints:
Santa Barbara, ay, Virgen,
Ay, Dios Mio!

The neighbors wrote
to her grown children in New York
that the daily water she was pumping
was spilling over her bare feet
like the thirteen afterbirths that had soaked them pain-red

so many years before;
concerned that her cracked brown fingers,
out of sight of her filmy eyes,
would set fires.
Ana y Colo's children,
like migrating geese,
had flown north, following
in each other's wake
and there was no one left
to fetch the water.
Though they loved their parents,
one by one they had departed,
falling victim to the lure
of exotic lands.

Upon hearing of her derangement
these expatriates pooled
their piecework pesos
and insisted Colo send them Ana
so they could care for her.
He resisted following, at first,
but her absence tugged
like the undertow of Caribbean waves
causing him to lose his balance
and follow reluctantly, inexorably.

Sometimes she'd forget
that Colo was her husband
and she'd shriek in terror
for Elisa, her daughter,
to rescue her from the man in bed
whose only obsession must be do her harm,
her lunacy resurrecting girlhood fears.

Ana's uproar was Colo's despair.
His knotted entrails would sink
like crabs disappearing into muddy flats.

The cruel camera, like a judge
ruling evidence inadmissible,
omits testimony of a time
when Colo's lizard green eyes
danced *merengues*;
his fruit-vendor hands played dominoes
under the constellations;
his *Boricua* passion
fell in love with his
Anita. The camera only intimates
that with his world so freshly buried
he will be soon to follow.

Li Min Mo

AFTERLIFE

We gather in my sister's
apartment to get ready to go
to my mother's funeral, and
take turns washing up in her
small narrow bathroom.
I close the door and come
face to face with a calendar,
each of September's boxes filled
with notes written neatly in
pencil—mother's last breath
sustained by a teaspoon of
pear juice, two tablets of
pain killers, half a cup of
almond pudding, one a.m.
pill time, three a.m. bath . . .

The last countdown, my
sister had awakened to cradle
Mother's cancerous body in
her arms, she forced liquid
into Mother's shrunken
mouth, washed her feet.
"Mother, don't walk away,"
she cried out to the night.
Lifting the stiffening body,
quickly removing the house
dress, she wrapped a purple
silk blouse around the bones,
then a red wool jacket, later
we put roses around her feet,
a pink quilt . . .

I'm sailing through this
spirited journey to eternity,

my fingers crawl like worms
through a pile of dead leaves,
I can feel the scissors my sister
used to cut Mother's house
dress apart. Each limb, each
side falls into this last box,
this unmeasurable space
connects me to breath, to
touch, to a multitude of voices
shrieking inside for the sky.

Aura Luz Sanchez

THE APPARITION

The room became as peaceful
as the mirror surface of a breezeless sea.
Negri's ears perked up
like cone-shaped party hats
while I, mournfully rummaging
through the old garments of our life,
unfolded the remnants
of those last few days together,
meandered on to our trip in Barcelona,
to our wedding.

Absorbed in the gauzy wrappings
of my mourning
I failed to notice her at first.
She wore a pink dress
with big white flowers and stood
where she always said
her own mother used to come and visit.
Her eyes, inscrutable ellipses, were
bailiffs to transcendental secrets.

I could not speak!
my words scurried like frightened kittens
hiding beneath my tongue.
I could not ask
if heaven was the field of wildflowers
she had dreamt one night it was;
we could only smile.

ELENA HARAP

TALK TO US ABOUT SALVATION
After a visit to Kakamega Christ Church, Kenya, July 1985

Note: *Shamba*, Swahili for a cultivated field;
here refers to a vegetable garden.

The Mothers' Union said,
"Talk to us about Salvation,"
but luckily
we had to catch a bus
before the meeting started.

Salvation must be something
I am supposed to comprehend
but I do not. I know something of the
phenomenon of saving things—
rubber bands, for instance,
should not be thrown away
but hung on a particular nail
in the kitchen.
Addresses from Christmas cards
should also be saved
and the wishbones of chickens.

In the House of All-Creation
so far I have been a rubber band, a return
address, a dried-out wishbone,
as have you.
"Praise the Lord!" the
Mothers' Union cries in chorus.

Dear Sisters, my words of praise
are untrained. It appears that I've been
saved, if by that we mean
I have survived,

in order to continue learning
how to praise, in order
to pursue the fulfillment
about which you would like
me to testify.

The joy of your harmonious
voices heals and disturbs me.

O good friends, my gospel tells me
that God is not a person,
that the power sustaining
us outbraves He and She
and resides in those who
stay away as much as
in those who attend.

I want to go on stretching;
I trust that All-Creation
will let me return some day
to these green hills and red-muddy roads,
papayas growing by the kitchen door,
maize in the *shamba*.
I believe in the maturing of wishes.

Amen?
It is silent, soundless the appearance of words
from this moving pen, the
service is over, the Mothers
in their blue dresses and head-ties
are somewhere else. We all
wake up in different rooms
in Nairobi
in Boston
in Kakamega
in the beating house of survival
in the daily awe.